PRAISE FOR MANA
FAST TRACK

'onathan ai ... is about getting things done, with clarity of vision and direction and building and motivating an effective team.

Mark Higson, Managing Director, Royal Mail

An important addition to the wealth of books around management theory – this is a very succinct, easily digestible summary of management principles packed with useful real-life examples and management and diagnostic tools that can easily be applied by the reader. Highly recommended for all new managers, promoted managers and simply for those wishing to sharpen up their current skill set.

Roger Smith, Head of EMEA Supply Chain, Pfizer

An immensely readable and involving approach to a whole range of critical management issues. The focus on creating value is important; we all need to be able to step back and analyse our activities in terms of their value-add and how we can maximise the impact of our efforts. As a pragmatic, real-world guide, this book will help managers to understand how they can shape and drive their career in corporate environments.

Peter Baxter, CEO of Old Mutual Asset Managers

This is a really usable book on management. It is good, readable stuff and very accessible – it works on every level. It has a sense of practicality and pragmatism that adds so much more than the usual heavy-duty theories and fads.

Ceri Green, Global Medical Affairs
Director of Danone Medical Nutrition

Jonathan Mowll has played a key role in developing my management team into an effective unit suited to the demands of 21st century business. To use his words: 'successful management does not just happen'. In this easy-reading book, the authors give a clear guide to climbing the management ladder quickly and effectively. It's a terrific toolkit.

Stephen Bourne, Chief Executive, Cambridge University Press

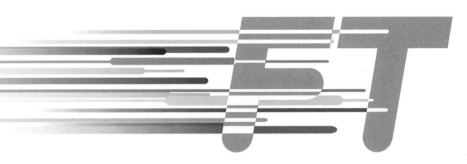

FAST TRACK TO SUCCESS
MANAGING

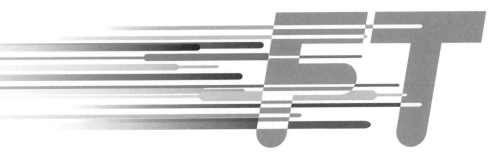

FAST TRACK TO SUCCESS

MANAGING

CHRISTOPHER O'NEILL &
JONATHAN MOWLL

Financial Times
Prentice Hall
is an imprint of

Harlow, England • London • New York • Boston • San Francisco • Toronto • Sydney • Singapore • Hong Kong
Tokyo • Seoul • Taipei • New Delhi • Cape Town • Madrid • Mexico City • Amsterdam • Munich • Paris • Milan

PEARSON EDUCATION LIMITED

Edinburgh Gate
Harlow CM20 2JE
Tel: +44 (0)1279 623623
Fax: +44 (0)1279 431059
Website: www.pearsoned.co.uk

First published in Great Britain in 2010

ISBN: 978-0-273-73290-7

British Library Cataloguing-in-Publication Data
A catalogue record for this book is available from the British Library

Library of Congress Cataloging-in-Publication Data
O'Neill, Chris.
   Fast track to success : managing / Chris O'Neill and Jonathan Mowll.
-- 1st ed.
      p. cm.
   Includes index.
   ISBN 978-0-273-73290-7 (pbk.)
   1. Management--Vocational guidance. 2. Leadership. I. Mowll,
Jonathan. II. Title.
   HD30.19.O54 2010
   658.0023--dc22

                                                 2010026322

10 9 8 7 6 5 4 3 2 1
14 13 12 11 10

Series text design by Design Deluxe
Typeset in 10/15 Swis Lt by 30
Printed by Ashford Colour Press Ltd, Gosport.

For Julie

Christopher O'Neill

For Lydia

Jonathan Mowll

CONTENTS

THE FAST TRACK WAY

Everything you need to accelerate your career

The best way to fast track your career as a manager is to fast track the contribution you and your team make to your organisation and for your team to be successful in as public a way as possible. That's what the Fast Track series is about. The Fast Track manager delivers against performance expectations, is personally highly effective and efficient, develops the full potential of their team, is recognised as a key opinion leader in the business, and ultimately progresses up the organisation ahead of their peers.

You will benefit from the books in the Fast Track series whether you are an ambitious first-time team leader or a more experienced manager who is keen to develop further over the next few years. You may be a specialist aiming to master every aspect of your chosen discipline or function, or simply be trying to broaden your awareness of other key management disciplines and skills. In either case, you will have the motivation to critically review yourself and your team using the tools and techniques presented in this book, as well as the time to stop, think and act on areas you identify for improvement.

Do you know what you need to know and do to make a real difference to your performance at work, your contribution to your company and your blossoming career? For most of us, the honest answer is 'Not really, no'. It's not surprising then that most of us never reach our full potential. The innovative Fast Track series gives you exactly what you need to speed up your progress and become a high performance manager in all the areas of the business that matter. Fast Track is not just another 'How to' series. Books on selling tell you how to win sales but not how to move from salesperson to sales manager. Project management software enables you to plan detailed tasks but doesn't improve the quality of your project management thinking and business performance. A marketing book tells you about the principles of marketing but not how to lead a team of marketers. It's not enough.

Specially designed features in the Fast Track books will help you to see what you need to know and to develop the skills you need to be successful. They give you:

→ the information required for you to shine in your chosen function or skill – particularly in the Fast Track top ten;

→ practical advice in the form of Quick Tips and answers to FAQs from people who have been there before you and succeeded;

→ state of the art best practice as explained by today's academics and industry experts in specially written Expert Voices;

→ case stories and examples of what works and, perhaps more importantly, what doesn't work;

→ comprehensive tools for accelerating the effectiveness and performance of your team;

→ a framework that helps you to develop your career as well as produce terrific results.

Fast Track is a resource of business thinking, approaches and techniques presented in a variety of ways – in short, a complete performance support environment. It enables managers to build careers from their first tentative steps into management all the way up to becoming a business director – accelerating the performance of their team and their career. When you use the Fast Track approach with your team it provides a common business language and structure, based on best business practice. You will benefit from the book whether or not others in the organisation adopt the same practices; indeed if they don't, it will give you an edge over them. Each Fast Track book blends hard practical advice from expert practitioners with insights and the latest thinking from experts from leading business schools.

The Fast Track approach will be valuable to team leaders and managers from all industry sectors and functional areas. It is for ambitious people who have already acquired some team leadership skills and have realised just how much more there is to know.

If you want to progress further you will be directed towards additional learning and development resources via an interactive Fast Track website, **www.Fast-Track-Me.com**. For many, these books therefore become the first step in a journey of continuous development. So, the Fast Track approach gives you everything you need to accelerate your career, offering you the opportunity to develop your knowledge and skills, improve your team's performance, benefit your organisation's progress towards its aims and light the fuse under your true career potential.

ABOUT THE AUTHORS

JONATHAN MOWLL is a founding director of Curo Consulting – a business that has grown over the last ten years to become a leading strategic adviser to the pharmaceutical sector, as well as delivering cutting-edge leadership development. His skill lies in developing powerful working relationships with clients and using simple, transferable management techniques to help clients grow their businesses. Jonathan gained extensive management and leadership experience running operations in Grand Metropolitan, Nestlé and Gillette before working as a successful strategy consultant at Kepner-Tregoe. He holds a PhD in microbiology.

CHRISTOPHER O'NEILL is managing director of Curo Consulting. He specialises in strategic consulting projects, delivering measurable business benefits in complex environments. With a background in articulating and executing strategy, Chris has gained an outstanding reputation as a results-driven pragmatist – working with management teams to deliver change in fast-moving operational environments while maintaining an appreciation of the upper-level priorities and drivers. Prior to entering consulting, Chris spent 12 years in sales and marketing management, in areas as diverse as food manufacturing, engineering and management information systems (MIS). Chris has a degree in modern languages from Liverpool University.

A WORD OF THANKS FROM THE AUTHORS

We would like to thank the following for their generous contributions to this book.

→ **Liz Gooster, Pearson**. There are many exciting new ideas in the publishing world at present, but without an enthusiastic champion, most will simply die a slow death. Liz had the confidence to commission the Fast Track series and associated web-tool on behalf of the Pearson Group at a time when other publishers were cutting back on non-core activities. She has remained committed to its success – providing direction, challenge and encouragement as and when required.

→ **Ken Langdon**. As well as being a leading author in his own right, Ken has worked with all the Fast Track authors to bring a degree of rigour and consistency to the series. As each book has developed, he has been a driving force behind the scenes, pulling the detailed content for each title together in the background – working with an equal measure of enthusiasm and patience!

→ **Mollie Dickenson**. Mollie has a background in publishing and works as a research manager at Henley Business School, and has been a supporter of the project from its inception. She has provided constant encouragement and challenge, and is, as always, an absolute delight to work with.

→ **Critical readers**. As the Fast Track series evolved, it was vital that we received constant challenge and input from other experts and from critical readers.

→ **Professor David Birchall**. David has worked to identify and source Expert Voice contributions from international academic and business experts in each Fast Track title. David is co-author of the Fast Track *Innovation* book and a leading academic author in his own right, and has spent much of the last 20 years heading up the research programme at Henley Business School – one of the world's top ten business schools.

Our expert team

Last but not least, we are grateful for the contributions made by experts from around the world in each of the Fast Track titles.

EXPERT	TOPIC	BUSINESS SCHOOL/ COMPANY
Professor John Burgoyne	Network theory and its usefulness in management, leadership, organisation and the development of all of these (p. 17)	School of Management, Lancaster University
Dr Peter Verdegem	Best-in-class stakeholder advocacy development (p. 29)	Danone Medical Nutrition
Professor Carol Print	Managing by means of budgets (p. 98)	Henley Business School, University of Reading
Ms Veronique Bourée	Virtual leadership – a strategic imperative (p. 115)	IBM
Professor Malcolm Higgs	What does it take to lead change successfully? (p. 133)	University of Southampton, School of Management
Professor David Olson	Models and frameworks for evaluating risks (p. 160)	University of Nebraska–Lincoln
Professor Chris Mabey	Management development: how much is explained by culture? (p.179)	Birmingham Business School, University of Birmingham
Professor George Tovstiga	Idea management (p. 198)	Henley Business School, University of Reading

MANAGING FAST TRACK

Management – the key to creating corporate Value

The heat is on! You may have noticed, but life in the workplace is not getting any easier. 'Value' is the new business mantra – we all need to deliver measurable, sustainable value. Businesses are striving for ever-increasing sales and the pressure on profits is even greater. Whether it is above the line or below the line, value is being wrought out of every sinew, fibre and function of a business. From HR and IT to supply chain, production, marketing, sales and beyond, the need to deliver value is now an unavoidable imperative and it is coupled with a need to be able to demonstrate and capitalise on this value. Each business must convince major stakeholders to keep backing the corporate vision in the sure-fire knowledge that this will prove a vehicle for increasing returns in a highly competitive environment.

How can this be done on a sustainable basis? Who will do it? Who will do it most effectively? The respective answers are: through better, more systematic, management; managers at all levels; Fast Track managers who, armed with the right tools, self-belief and attitude, will succeed in delivering sustainable value. In the process, they will be noticed and accelerated through the organisation. Any business worth its salt – and with an eye to future growth – will value and reward the deliverers of strategic and operational value.

Diversity of management approach – different but equal

Fast Track managers deploy a whole range of skills and no two styles are the same. Having respect for different approaches is vital in terms of acceptance of cultural and human diversity and, in fostering and promoting different intellectual approaches. It represents a key way in which people must be allowed to be different. Some will adopt a studied, considerate approach to decision-making; others will be more gung-ho. Some will involve the team and peers; others will go it alone. The commonality between the differing styles of managing is that all managers will make mistakes (some more than others, admittedly), but the Fast Track managers will make fewer and the way they handle mistakes will be better – learning from history and striving to be better next time.

Of all the different approaches, one of the hardest to reconcile is the way in which different managers handle the concept of value. Any approach that fails to get to grips with the key areas of value that a role or function must deliver is a flawed approach. Having overcome this hurdle, any working approach then has to deliver and maximise the impact of any value-creating activities. If your approach does this, you will be on the right road.

The importance of being practical

It is not enough to talk a good game. The only currency that is respected universally in the modern business environment is that of demonstrable results. Whatever the approach, any manager needs to understand the metrics of success and determine how these will be delivered and improved – boiling it down to first principles.

→ Who will do what and when?

→ How will this add value?

→ How will results and progress be verified before it is too late?

Many businesses and managers can tend to overengineer the mechanics of delivery. Like all good things, though, the best are typically the simplest.

Embedding management

If management is about creating value – then it is worth understanding that value is not a fleeting concept but a long-term enhancement of the corporate effectiveness and ability to thrive. In this context, it is logical also that driving effective management is not a one-off activity – landing a single project or the delivery of an event or winning a single piece of business or a great new product, for example. Effective management has to be embedded in the culture and working ethos of a business. The Fast Track manager must also develop an approach that will not only see him through the next crisis but also serve as a flexible blueprint for becoming the long-term value creator who will be a key part of the business management team for years to come, moving up through the corporate structure, seeking out new challenges and reinforcing a new business paradigm. Given a clear vision and tangible metrics, success and value can be managed, created and delivered.

Let's think about management and how it links to your business. As an organisation grows, its management demands will change: a small, sole trader business will have quite different needs from those of a multinational organisation. The basic elements of any business, however, are fundamentally the same, it's just the relative emphasis that changes. So, whether you are operating in a small business or a very large one or applying this thinking to part of a business, the following rules apply.

Central to all organisations are the **business processes**. These are where value is added to some input from a supplier before the item or service is passed on to a customer. Business processes could be the core of an organisation's activity, such as manufacturing tins of food or managing cash movements in customers' bank accounts, or they can be equally vital support processes, such as invoice processing or sales. Management is about organising everything in and around those business processes to make sure that the right amount of value is created efficiently.

At the front line, those in **operational management** take or are given information from the business processes. This comes in the form of **reports**, which may be verbal, paper, electronic, dials and so on. Managers react to this information and make changes to the business processes to improve performance. This is fundamentally what a manager does in any business.

Of course, 'making changes to improve' can look different depending on the nature of your organisation, but it will generally always impact certain areas of the business and usually managing the *people* aspects, the **internal environment**. Within this, you will be managing **skills** and **capabilities**, making sure that individuals have the necessary skills to do the work required and there are enough or not too many of them to get the work done effectively and efficiently. You will be motivating (or demotivating) them via the **reward system**, which might, in some cases, be giving them a financial bonus for good performance, but, as you will see later in this book, other forms of recognition may be equally or more valid. In larger organisations, **communication** will become a more significant challenge, as you endeavour to keep everyone working in the same direction and ensure that they are informed about the way the business is going and how they are contributing to that. **Technology** is increasingly a way to make the business processes more efficient and effective, improve the flow of process information to all those who need it and make people's jobs more fulfilling. Alongside all of this, you will also need to manage human interactions in the form of **meetings**, in which decisions and plans are made and problems resolved.

This aspect of the manager's job is about continuous improvement. It is about observing and reacting and making, often small, changes to nudge the business process in the right direction. Of course, a manager's job doesn't end there: management is also about **leadership** and **strategy**, the art of setting clear goals for the future and inspiring people to strive for these goals. These elements of management are often harder to pin down and managers who do this well may be regarded as having a 'natural' talent for it. Sure, some people have more natural charisma than others, but, as you will discover later in this book, there are different ways to lead and plenty of skills that *all* managers can learn and adopt to become better leaders and strategists.

In the end, all businesses need excellent managers and, while managing across a range of factors is challenging and demanding, the rewards to the organisation and therefore to the excellent Fast Track manager are significant.

HOW TO USE THIS BOOK

Fast Track books present a collection of the latest tools, techniques and advice to help build your team and your career. Use this table to plan your route through the book.

PART	OVERVIEW
About the authors	A brief overview of the authors, their background and their contact details
A **Awareness**	*This first part gives you an opportunity to gain a quick overview of the topic and to reflect on your current effectiveness*
1 *Management in a nutshell*	A brief overview of Management and a series of frequently asked questions to bring you up to speed quickly
2 *Management audit*	Simple checklists to help identify strengths and weaknesses in your team and your capabilities
B **Business Fast Track**	*Part B provides tools and techniques that may form part of the integrated Management framework for you and your team*
3 *Fast Track top ten*	Ten tools and techniques used to help you implement a sustainable approach to Management based on the latest best practice
4 *Technologies*	A review of the latest information technologies used to improve effectiveness and efficiency of Management activities
5 *Implementing change*	A detailed checklist to identify gaps and to plan the changes necessary to implement your goals
C **Career Fast Track**	*Part C focuses on you, your leadership qualities and what it takes to get to the top*
6 *The first ten weeks*	Recommended activities when starting a new role in project management, together with a checklist of useful facts to know
7 *Leading the team*	Managing change, building your team and deciding your leadership style
8 *Getting to the top*	Becoming a Management professional, getting promoted and becoming a director – what does it take?
D **Director's toolkit**	*The final part provides more advanced tools and techniques based on industry best practice*
Toolkit	Advanced tools and techniques used by senior managers
Glossary	Glossary of terms

FAST-TRACK-ME.COM

Before reading this book, why not start by visiting our companion website www.Fast-Track-Me.com? This is a custom-designed, highly interactive online resource that addresses the needs of the busy manager by providing access to ideas and methods that will

improve individual and team performance quickly, and develop both your skills and your career.

As well as giving you access to cutting-edge business knowledge across a range of key topics – including the subject of this book – Fast-Track-Me.com will enable you to stop and think about what you want to achieve in your chosen career and where you want to take your team. By doing this, it will provide a context for reading and give you extra information and access to a range of interactive features.

The site in general is packed with valuable features, such as:

→ **The Knowledge Cube**. The K-Cube is a two-dimensional matrix presenting Fast Track features from all topics in a consistent and easy-to-use way – providing ideas, tools and techniques in a single place, anytime, anywhere. This is a great way to delve in and out of business topics quickly.

→ **The Online Coach**. The Online Coach is a toolkit of fully inter-active business templates in MS Word format that allow Fast-Track-Me.com users to explore specific business methods (strategy, ideas, projects etc.) and learn from concepts, case examples and other resources according to your preferred learning style.

→ **Business Glossary**. The Fast Track Business Glossary pro-vides a comprehensive list of key words associated with each title in the Fast Track series together with a plain English defini-tion – helping you to cut through business jargon.

To access even more features, carry out self-diagnostic tests and develop your own personal profile, simply log-in and register – then click on My FastTrack to get started! Give yourself the Fast Track Health Check now.

My FastTrack

These are the different areas you'll discover in the My FastTrack area.

My HealthCheck

How effective is your team compared with industry 'best practices'? Find out using a simple Red, Amber, Green (RAG) scale.

After identifying areas of concern, you can plan for their resolution using a personal 'Get2Green' action plan.

My Get2Green Actions

What are the specific actions you and your team will implement in order to 'Get2Green' and improve performance? Log, prioritise and monitor your action points in the My Get2Green Action Plan area to help you plan for future success – fast.

My Career

Reflect on your current role and plan your future career – how prepared are you for future success?

Fast-Track-Me.com provides the busy manager with access to the latest thinking, techniques and tools at their fingertips. It can also help answer some of the vital questions managers are asking themselves today.

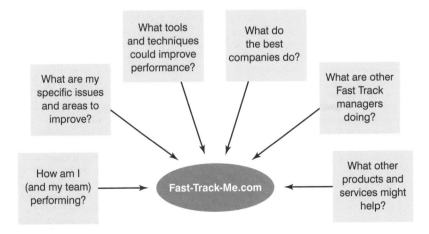

Don't get left behind: log on to **www.Fast-Track-Me.com** now to get your career on the fast track.

PART A

AWARENESS

This book introduces a sustainable approach to being a manager, aimed at keeping you, your team and your organisation at the forefront of high performance, thus contributing towards the future of all three. The starting point is to gain a quick understanding of what professional management is and what it is not, and to be aware of your own and your team's capabilities in this area right now. For this reason, we will ask you a number of questions that will reveal where you and your team need to improve if you are to perform to a world-class standard.

'Know yourself' was the motto above the doorway of the Oracle at Delphi and is a wise thought. It means that you must do an open and honest self-audit as you start on the process of building your part of the business into a high-performing unit.

The stakes are high. Good management is at the heart of success in this global, competitive marketplace. Your team, therefore, needs to be performing effectively and you need to be a good leader. Poor leadership and poor team effectiveness will make failure likely. An effective team poorly led will sap the team's energy and lead in the long term to failure through their leaving for a better environment or becoming less effective through lack of motivation. Leading an ineffective team well does not prevent the obvious conclusion that an ineffective team will not thrive. So, looking at the figure below, how do you make sure that you and your team are in the top right-hand box – an innovative and effective team with an excellent leader? That's what this book is about and this part shows you how to discover your and your team's starting point.

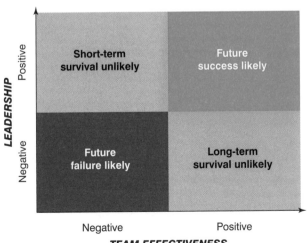

MANAGEMENT IN A NUTSHELL

Starting with the basics

Just what is management?

Business books cover management very extensively – strewn with a great many theories, models and practices. It is unquestionably important as businesses ultimately depend on good management to deliver results. The concept of management is actually quite simple.

→ Management in all businesses is simply the act of getting people together to accomplish desired goals and objectives.

→ Management comprises planning, organising, staffing, leading, directing, facilitating and controlling an organisation or unit for the purpose of accomplishing a goal.

Why is management increasingly important?

Over the last 15 years, there have been three major trends.

→ Maintaining competitiveness has become a relentless drive towards improved efficiency and effectiveness. Just think of the things that cost relatively or even actually less than they did 15 years ago: clothes, electronic goods, white goods, toys, and we could go on. Also, consumers are getting better products with better after-sales service. The drive, therefore, to improve service and reduce costs has led to changes in how organisations go about their tasks. Cycles of change have become shorter and the pace of change ever greater. This requires considerably more effort from managers as they seek to prioritise and provide focus while maintaining control and momentum and marshalling the various resources now open to them.

→ Companies face increasing expectations from their customers and consumers: they have got used to continuous improvement in what the business world offers them. They are better informed about possibilities because of access to information – in part fuelled by the internet. This offers opportunities for product/price comparisons that were impossible in the days when the only way you could get that information was from biased advertisements and walking round the shops. Put simply, they want more for less, and they want it faster. They won't accept mediocrity because if we can't deliver, someone else will.

→ Finally comes globalisation: no matter how big or small you are, you are now competing in a global market. The corner shop, struggling with higher prices because it lacks the buying muscle of the big national retailers, is now also competing head-to-head with sellers on e-Bay, and with offers of home-delivery.

The onus is now on the management of businesses to deliver results from the resources and teams they have available to them. Coordinating and controlling are no longer sufficient. Managers now have to get more out of their teams than the sum of individuals' efforts; they have to inspire and challenge and help people to focus on what matters.

QUICK TIP DELIVER ON YOUR PROMISES
If you say you are going to do something, *do it*. If for whatever reason you cannot deliver, warn the affected parties. Explain the issues and reschedule. Failure to do this will ruin your reputation; doing it well will ensure that you are seen as a responsible and trustworthy business partner.

The pitfalls: obstacles to successful managers and successful management

The importance of successful management to the future success of a company is hard to ignore. Successful management does not just happen, though – it is the output of a select level of people who are able to martial resources to deliver the business strategy. As a Fast Track manager, you will have to acquire and deploy a wide and diverse skill set in a practical, results-focused environment.

Let's make a panoramic start by looking first at what can go wrong. This should make you think about particular areas in your business or team where one or more of these problems occur and focus your attention on fixing them. Then we will look at a number of frequently asked questions to finish off this rapid introduction to the topic.

1 **The business and its management do not really support change.** Lots of organisations talk a good game when it comes to strategic renewal. The strategic vision is well articulated and the media is impressed with the new energy and sense of purpose. In the real world, however, realising a vision requires a change in working practices and culture that many organisations find hard to get off the ground. There is often little evidence that senior management has the stomach for root and branch revision of business processes. Think of government and the NHS – lots of fine words, but will the internal bureaucracy ever really change?

2 **Why bother – small cog in a big wheel.** As a manager trying to get traction in a big organisation, how can the actions of one person really make a difference? Faced with an organisation that may operate across many functions in many geographies and with potentially tens of thousands of co-workers, for some it is hard to imagine how they can effect meaningful change as customers and suppliers already have a fixed opinion of the business and co-workers are often entrenched, transitory or virtual. Just doing your job well in such circumstances can be a real challenge – anything beyond this is simply not realistic.

3 Poor communication. 'Send three and four-pence, we're going to a dance!' ... or was it, 'Send reinforcements, we're going to advance!'? Effective communication is *critical* to success. Many businesses fail to communicate strategy and, even when they do, they often forget to communicate the implications of the strategy to internal people on the ground. Quite apart from this, given the welter of untargeted corporate communications in today's working world (emails, conference calls, pronouncements from HR and other corporate propaganda), it is amazing that the busy manager can ever sort the wheat from the chaff. Filtering out the critical stuff that will help to make a difference can be a lottery.

QUICK TIP *SIMPLE COMMUNICATION*
People are busy and haven't got time for complicated messages. When you know what your vision is, turn it into a single phrase or sentence and tell people regularly.

---

4 Rotation – panacea or pain the neck? Like Total Football, everybody is expected to be able to do everything. People are shifted around organisations in an attempt to give them experience of each area. The idea is great in principle – it gives people a flavour of different functions, what they do, what pressures they face – but it is sometimes taken too far. A manager is parachuted into a new function (such as the supply chain or production) and suddenly asked to make big decisions. The results can be chaotic and very damaging – for the manager as well as the business.

5 Managers who aren't managers. Many managers are often given this exalted position because they did well in their previous functional roles. For example, almost all sales managers were great salespeople. Not all of them are great managers, though. They may just be poor management material, but, quite often, the reason for their underperformance is that they are also still being asked to do the *old* day job – managing client accounts and making targets. Quite often – given that this is their history and comfort zone – they focus on the day job rather than their new management responsibilities. Unsurprisingly, the function tends not to move forward as a whole in such circumstances.

6 **Operations v. strategy.** Many managers *want* to deliver change but can't because they are constantly being measured by short-term targets and keeping internal and external stakeholders happy. Doing the day job requires 100 per cent devotion, so how on earth can someone focus on developing and delivering against long-term strategic targets when the phone is ringing and a PowerPoint is due explaining why last quarter's figures were so wide of the mark?

7 **Other people.** We all have to manage the people we are given. In an ideal world, a manager's team would be capable of delivering to our requirements with little need for management, enabling the manager to move on and deliver strategic improvement. Quite often this is not the case – new hires and long-term underperformers litter the landscape and, while some have great potential, others are no more than millstones. Either way, each group demands time and effort and can sap the energy of even the most dedicated manager.

8 **No follow-through.** The road to hell is paved with best intentions. Many businesses set out aiming for greatness but the real world intervenes to knock everything off course. This is an inevitability in a working environment; there is little one can do about resignations, corporate takeovers and other acts of god but such events should represent a blip or hiccup not a stake through the heart. The issue here is one of follow-though – or lack thereof. If there is no system of tracking and monitoring progress, or if such a system is peripheral or secondary to other business drivers, then when stormy winds blow a strategy off course, when the winds subside, there is often rarely a backward glance to the old goals, instead there's a headlong rush into new futures. Goals are not realised and, worse still, this cycle of non-delivery repeats itself as night follows day.

9 **Blame culture.** The fear of failure can stop a business dead in its tracks. Criticism of people's best efforts is a constant

problem in some businesses. It is sometimes personal, but, even if it is data-driven and 'fair', the apportionment of blame to somebody who has tried and failed does not just demotivate that person but is also seen and felt by all and its effect is pervasive, stopping people from trying new things and, ultimately, cutting off the oxygen of innovation. Mistakes clearly cost money, but *not* daring to change or try anything new is likely to cost a hell of a lot more.

10 **No experience – and no support to grow.** It is hard work being a manager. Being a new manager is even harder and external support from the business is not just a hand-holding exercise required by ineffectual, naive managers but key to ongoing growth and success of the best mangers. Mentoring, coaching, development and support are recognised by many companies as key enablers. Many simply don't invest in this area and even those that do can sometimes offer this support as a tick box exercise. Outsourcing support and management development is a risky strategy – it can work, but, if it is not joined up and supported by the efforts of senior management, young, high-potential managers will see it as a cop-out. The demotivation can be real and devastating for the managers and the business. It is a key driver of high churn and the loss of good people.

These potential pitfalls can be addressed in isolation or as part of an integrated framework, as presented in the Director's toolkit in Section D.

 **CASE STORY RESPECT THROUGH UNDERSTANDING,
ALBERTO'S STORY**

Narrator Alberto had been given the job of plant general manager in a factory in south east Asia. This was a far cry from his background as a sales manager, but he had been successful to date, due to his ability to think and act differently – he could think outside the box.

Context This global component supplier was successfully opening new markets in Asia and had decided to shift the manufacture of a core range products to the region to capitalise on local production costs and supply chain efficiencies.

Issue Alberto's plant was used for commodity business – long runs of single products. The new portfolio required a great deal more expertise and flexibility. The efficiencies that the group was targeting also extended to improving working practices. In a country where religion played a key part in people's lives, the demands of the business were potentially at odds with this and unrest threatened Alberto's hopes of achieving change. As a new manager, he could not simply order people to do what he asked. As if to reinforce the cultural challenge facing Alberto, he discovered his plant contained a mosque that was being used by the local villagers. During peak production times he was more than a little surprised to see women, children and sheep drifting across busy areas of the plant, apparently on their way to worship. From a health and safety perspective, this was clearly unacceptable, but, in terms of community and worker relationships, what could he do?

Solution Alberto built a mosque! Just outside the plant. This enabled workers to observe their religious practices without compromising the production environment (the other nearest mosque was nearly 7 km away) and it increased the standing of the company within the local community. Productivity rose and the workers gained real respect for a manager who appeared to respond to their needs ahead of those of the company.

Learning To drive performance, Alberto needed buy-in from a workforce that had a different cultural take on the world. Alberto figured that he needed to respect their culture, not give 'corporate messages'. Alberto knew that respect is earned, not given, and real respect is achieved by doing something that is both valid and significant. Building a mosque wasn't just done to satisfy corporate health and safety rules; it was done because Alberto understood what mattered to his workforce. The people didn't want money or extra holidays, but somebody who was prepared to understand what really mattered. The key learning here is that you don't give people what you *think* they want – ask them and try to deliver according to their *real* needs and motivators.

What is management? – frequenty asked questions

Management is an oft-used term, but what does it actually mean? The following table provides quick answers to some of the most frequently asked questions on the topic of management. Use this as a way of gaining a quick overview.

FAQ 1 What is management?	1 It is the art and science of coordinating people and activities in order to deliver against a common objective. In the commercial environment, management is concerned with the delivery of business value to customers and shareholders. Management is often seen as a controlling process, but it is also about setting visions and goals for the future, building on creativity and getting the best from people and teams.
FAQ 2 Our products are great, our markets are buoyant. Why does good management matter?	2 We live in a changing world. What works today will almost certainly not be state of the art tomorrow. The environment within which a business operates is fluid – there are constant changes in markets and competition. Good managers will think about the future, make plans and respond to any changes they see around them. Done properly, management helps position the organisation to take advantage of the changing landscape. The alternative to management is trusting to luck – it *may* come off, but it is no basis for building a long-term business (or your career!)
FAQ 3 How do I start managing a team that I have been a member of for the last couple of years?	3 If you're the one who gets the promotion from within the team, you will be pleased to have beaten the competition, but also potentially nervous about managing your previous peers. There are some golden rules for this. First, develop some detachment – it's nice to be friendly, but, if you're to do this job well, your old friends will have to get used to a slightly different you. Second, don't have favourites. Third, be objective and fact-based in your interactions with the team. Finally, use rigorous management by objectives – that is, set and review measurable objectives annually and review individuals' progress monthly.
FAQ 4 Matrix or hierarchy – which is the best management structure?	4 Typically, a hierarchical structure is perceived as being appropriate where a business is simple and/or located in one place. It is sometimes regarded as the 'cleanest' way to make people accountable for the deliverables associated with their jobs. In more complex (often global) environments, you may have a regional and a functional line manager – a local HR manager may report to the local managing director *and* the central HR director, for example. This becomes the most effective way to ensure that the individual is driven by local needs and objectives while also adhering to global principles and strategy. The key to matrix working is that the strategic drivers of the different managers are clear, agreed and *not* in conflict. Sadly, this is often not the case.

FAQ 5 How are management and career progression linked?	5 Career progression is often an inevitable consequence of being good at your job. Quite often, for example, we see the best researcher being promoted to role of research manager. If promoted, you will need to develop the skills required to manage others *as well as* your own job and find the correct balance between the two. Sometimes, the best researcher doesn't make the best manager and, in some organisations, these people are rewarded with status and remuneration without typical management responsibilities.
FAQ 6 Is management something you can really learn or is it an innate ability?	6 Both! All individuals have strengths and weaknesses across the range of management capabilities. Some are good at numbers and structure; others are good with teams; yet others are charismatic and good communicators. The key to individual success is to understand and build on your strengths and recognise and improve on your weaknesses. Nobody is born the complete manager. The best managers are open, recognising that they will always have a lot to learn.
FAQ 7 How do you manage a poor performer?	7 First, be clear about expectations and measures. Do they know what's expected of them? Have they been given any training? Are you measuring their performance objectively? Second, make sure that they're encouraged to perform. Are they rewarded for good performance or penalised, such as given more work to do? Do they get positive feedback from customers/colleagues/ you? Third, review their performance regularly and coach them where they may be struggling. If none of this succeeds, you may have to resort to your organisation's disciplinary procedures, but always try the positive approach first.
FAQ 8 What is the difference between managing people and other aspects of business?	8 You can set targets and goals for each and manage progress accordingly, but, put quite simply, people have feelings, other aspects of business don't. This is obvious, but, in practice, it means that people need more time and a more flexible, personalised approach. The best managers devote time to profiling their key people and developing approaches to maximise their performance.
FAQ 9 How can I be recognised as a good manager?	9 Getting lost in the middle of a large organisation is not hard. For your career (and sanity), being recognised as a deliverer of value can be very important. Nobody likes a self-publicist, but, equally, if you have a good strategy, work out ways of sharing it with senior colleagues. When you have results, present these in a way that shows how your results will help others.

FAQ 10 What can go wrong in management?

10 Given that management covers a lot of bases, there are lots of opportunities to slip up (though following the advice in this book will set you up to succeed!) Good management, however, is not about avoiding mistakes at all costs. The best managers try things and learn from their mistakes. They figure out how to change their approach and behaviour to become stronger managers in the future. The biggest potential pitfall is to *not* stretch yourself as a manager.

FAQ 11 How do I benchmark my performance as a manager and is it important to do this?

11 To become an excellent manager, it is vital that you assess your ability against a benchmark and plan how you will learn and improve. The next chapter in this book gives you a set of objective criteria against which you can evaluate your performance. Also, don't just rely on your own views – see if you can get inputs from your boss, your peers and your reports (called **360° feedback**). Remember to repeat the benchmarking process and self-evaluation as you may have got better, which is great, but it will be important to know in which areas you can still develop.

FAQ 12 How do I select the right management style?

12 There is a whole range of management styles, from the democratic to the autocratic, with hundreds of styles in between and a few more at the edges. You need to select a style that fits with the needs of the business, your team and your own natural approach. Try not to be guided too much by your own comfort zone, but, equally, don't try to be what you are not!

FAQ 13 How do I avoid 'overcontrolling' or 'micromanaging' my team?

13 If you're asking this, you may have a natural tendency to manage every detail of your team's activities, checking as they go. There's a good chance that the people in your team will be frustrated by this. You will be undermining their confidence and spending so much time checking up on things that nothing gets done. There is a 'different horses for different courses' theme here, though: if your team members are new or inexperienced, it may be appropriate to work closely with them as they learn. As they grow in confidence, you can relax your style and delegate more responsibility. Of course, the opposite can happen and be equally disruptive – that is, you are naturally a laissez-faire delegator when what your team needs is close management and regular input. The trick is to get the balance right. Give the experts a long leash, work with the less experienced people until they are confident, then let them *go*!

FAQ 14 How do I find the time to manage my team and achieve my objectives?

14 The simple answer to this question is that *your* objectives are now your *team's* objectives. Most of your objectives should form the basis of the objectives you give your team. Once you have agreed these objectives with team members, remember to review performance regularly and adapt your management style (see FAQ 13). If you miss your routine of ticking things off the 'to do' list, adapt it to include management tasks that are 'forward-looking' and will improve the performance of the team. Include strategy-setting and performance management, for example, coaching and developing individuals, reviewing processes and meetings to optimise your department's performance and so on.

FAQ 15 What is the difference between management and managing expectations?

15 Management is about achieving common objectives. Managing expectations is about negotiating the realpolitik of corporate life and you cannot do the former without the latter. In the real world, the best-laid plans will often go awry, so building pragmatism into your up-front and ongoing communications will ensure that you don't end up with egg on your face when things don't quite go according to plan. Experienced business managers will offer you simplest advice when it comes to managing expectations: underpromise and overdeliver!

FAQ 16 What do I do if my line manager tells me to do my functional job (salesperson, for example) as opposed to my management role (sales manager, say)?

16 When the chips are down and your boss is looking to make the numbers for the quarterly board update, you may be told to go and do the job yourself. If your boss carries on doing this, it means that he or she still only really knows and accepts you for your functional performance. You are either not being an effective manager or not being *seen* to be an effective manager. Review your management goals and deliverables with your line manager and communicate your successes more effectively. Make your *management* results more 'indispensible' than your *functional* results by aligning them with your manager's broader needs, so he or she doesn't just look to you for results at quarter end!

FAQ 17 What management tools should be I be using?

17 If management is about controlling the journey to your goal, management *tools* may help you to plan, structure, deliver and monitor what you are doing. Designing templates that encourage consistent behaviours is a good start – word-processing and spreadsheets are good enablers but can fall into misuse. Web-tools can encourage greater consistency, but don't think tools alone are the answer. Show people how to use them – not just technically, but also how the tool will help and not be just another chore.

***FAQ 18** Should I be allocating a budget to management?*	18 You may need a budget for training, tools, coaching and consulting – all of which are key enablers of your management objectives – but it is important that these are seen as being aligned with strategic and operational deliverables. They are therefore more clearly identified as adding value and are less likely to be targeted when budgets are being squeezed.
***FAQ 19** Is managing people by targets likely to stifle creativity and results?*	19 In some industries there are 'perverse objectives', which govern a function but seem counterproductive to the business as a whole. For example, 'speed' (such as speed to market) is often a critical business factor. If one function is measured by speed and another by quality, however, there is likely to be conflict. You may see this when the product development team is measured on speed to market and the product may be substandard but the development team members get their bonus. This leaves sales with a product that, although first to market, does not meet the needs of that market and so sits on the shelf. You must ensure that all your teams' targets are aligned to drive results, intelligent thinking and creativity.
***FAQ 20** Management seems to be a series of the latest gimmicks. How do I avoid being conned by the latest fad?*	20 Management, quite rightly, is an evolving discipline. There will always be new thinking – some good, some questionable. As a forward-looking manager, it is important to be open to new thinking and techniques. The test is to evaluate and challenge what you see against three criteria. → Does it support my attempts to add value? → Is it common sense? If it seems a bit far-fetched, it probably will be! → Is it practical? If it is too complex and expensive, it may not be worth it.

QUICK TIP *DON'T TAKE NO FOR AN ANSWER*

Try to understand *why* somebody is saying no. It may be that the reason is something you can deal with (such as timing or lack of clarity on a goal). Even if the answer is *still* no, finding out why will be useful for further work with this person and may help when trying to get someone else's commitment.

Network theory and its usefulness in management, leadership, organisation and the development of all of these

Professor John Burgoyne School of Management, Lancaster University

This note sets out some of the basics of network theory (NT), then goes on to outline six ways in which it can be applied so as to understand and intervene in management, leadership and their development (MLOD).

The basics

The basic idea in NT is that the world can be thought of as being made up of nodes and links. The most obvious example is people as nodes and their relationships as links. Social network theory is about this and LinkedIn, Facebook and others are examples of everyday practices associated with this.

You can, however, move up, down and across from this.

→ Moving up, networks of people become groups, teams, departments that can be thought of as nodes in themselves, relating to each other in organisations and so on, up to industries, clusters, supply chains, sectors and on to nation states, the world and beyond.

→ Moving down, people can be thought of physiologically as networks or organs and psychologically as networks of subpersonalities and subidentities.

This up and down pattern we can call recursiveness as each node can be seen as a network internally and part of a bigger node externally.

→ Moving sideways, people and groups can have in their networks 'non-human actants', as they are called in actor network theory – that is, tools, computers, cars, houses and so on.

Networks can be 'naturally occurring', as in the evolution of many towns, cities or communities, or they can be 'contrived', by being planned, designed and managed, as in new towns and, for example, cancer, cardio and diabetes networks in the NHS.

The term **network** can be reserved for systems with relatively equal power and influence within or between nodes or for any situation where there are quite large power differences.

When the term network is used as an alternative to the idea of hierarchy of market as the main ways of arranging people and departments in organisations, then it is the former. In the other sense, hierarchies and markets are themselves networks with particular forms of relationship between the nodes.

Links, at any level of recursiveness, can be strong, weak or non-existent. Generally, as in our personal relationships, we can have a few strong links or many weak ones or both. It would be hard to have a large number of very close friends.

Six degrees of separation

It is said that you can reach anyone in the world through someone you know who knows someone and so on, within six such links.

Networks as a contemporary phenomenon

The term network has been of increasing interest and use recently. This is almost certainly down to IT and communications, the worldwide web and so on, and possibly a trend, perhaps with growing affluence, to less authoritarian relationships (hence, networks in the more egalitarian sense).

Applications

Here are six examples of applications of NT to MLOD. I have a list of over 100 more. In each case, I suggest that they can be used to *understand* situations, but also how to read or *diagnose* them and how to influence them, how to *intervene*.

1 Online communities of practice. This is a popular idea for thinking about how people work together and learn, individually and collectively, to improve the practice involved. Communities of practice can be naturally occurring or contrived. Often they start as the former and then someone thinks that they can improve them

by doing the latter. Sometimes the idea is used when designing new work arrangements from scratch. Often the people involved with a specific practice – drilling for oil, for example – are physically dispersed. In such situations, it is attractive for someone to link them up electronically to share experiences and lessons. This is a form of initiative often carried out under the heading of knowledge management.

2 **Stickiness.** It is said that organisations increasingly depend on knowledge and the development, acquisition and application of new knowledge. Stickiness is an idea applied in knowledge management theory. If an organisation is acquiring useful new knowledge from somewhere else, stickiness is a 'bad thing' – like treacle in a pipe, it travels badly. When knowledge gets to where it can be applied, stickiness is a 'good thing', because it needs to stick to its target in order to be used. Actually, it is more complicated than this. There is plenty of knowledge around, not all of it useful. In the ideal world, stickiness would be selective, both in transmission and at the target. We need non-stick pipes that make it easier for the useful knowledge to travel and non-stick targets so less useful knowledge slips off.

3 **Implosion, explosion and distortion.** When a network has strong internal links and weak external ones, it tends to implode. Members relate to each other and get cut off from the outside world. At the extreme, such networks become cults. Imploded networks are strongly bonded, but not good at learning to adapt to, or adapting, their environments. When a network has weak internal and strong external links, it tends to explode – that is, get pulled apart by the influences of its external stakeholders. At the extreme, such networks disintegrate. In my experience of NHS networks, diabetes ones, which are the ones that I have studied most, have a tendency to explode. Here, for example, the clinical members are pulled by the British Medical Council and their loyalties to their clinical colleagues, while the administrators are pulled by their Trust's chief executives. Often the networks have limited budgets and weak or non-existent internal leadership. Many networks, like a ball on top of a hill, have a tendency to roll one way or another. It is difficult to keep things in balance. Action learning is a good way of doing this as it bonds the group internally, but also supports them focusing on external challenges and external stakeholders. Distortion happens when one set of external stakeholders has stronger links with the network and its members than another set. Whether this is

a good or bad thing obviously depends on a values perspective. When, however, an NHS clinical network is more strongly pulled to the different professional associates of members, as opposed to patients, despite various initiatives for patient service and involvement, this is what happens.

4 **Markets, hierarchies and clans.** It is said that there are just these three options when it comes to organising, or designing, organisations. Like the three basic colours, they can be combined in different proportions to achieve different effects.

→ **Markets** are where business units buy and sell goods and services, perhaps with a final assembler putting together the overall product or service.

→ **Hierarchies**, we tend to know about – they are the ones that are mapped like an inverted family tree.

→ **Clans** are groups held together by shared beliefs and values. The term network, in the egalitarian sense, is sometimes used as an alternative to clans.

The pre-NHS health sector was a clan, run by the doctors. The NHS, as part of the Welfare State, introduced a State-regulated hierarchy. Recently, there have been attempts, with the purchaser/provider split, to introduce a significant element of market. The introduction of clinical networks can be seen as an attempt to get back some of the strengths of clan – or network in the egalitarian sense. Prior to Henry Ford, cars were made by a market mechanism. Wheels, carriages, engines and so on were made by different people who bought and sold bits from each other and one of them put the final thing together. Henry put it all under one roof, with the different units regulated by a hierarchical superstructure. More recently, large corporations, such as Ford, have attempted culture change programmes to acquire some of the virtues of clans. Mission and value statements are the sign of this, while targets, aims and objectives are signs of hierarchy.

5 **Social networks.** I have already mentioned these – Facebook, for example. Their use is certainly substantial and growing. From a business and personal point of view, the question is, how useful are they, other than for social and fun purposes (which are not to be sneezed at)? As far as I can see, organisations are confused as to whether to ban them or encourage their use from their corporate machines. Positive uses might be to draw in knowledge, build relationships with all the important stakeholders – owners/sponsors,

suppliers, markets, labour markets and 'neighbours'. Developing an audit tool for this could be a good idea.

6 **Inter-agency working.** This is a very popular approach, particularly in the public sector. It is seen as the way to deliver joined-up government and avoid the kinds of problems and crises that occur when things fall through the gaps between, for example, police, social work, local government, housing, health and education. It does seem particularly difficult to make it work in practice, however. There seem to be two approaches to developing and implementing a strategy for doing this. One is to design and micro-manage them in detail. This is often attempted in a collaborative and consultative way and frequently does not get beyond the sharing and discussion stage. The other approach is to put the enabling conditions in place and hope that it will emerge. It's like organising a party or a carnival – if you micromanage it, you can kill it, but, if you leave too much to natural emergence, nothing may happen or things may get out of hand.

EXPERT VOICE

MANAGEMENT AUDIT

In order to improve performance, you first need to understand what your starting point is, what your strengths and weaknesses are and how each will promote or limit what you can achieve. There are two levels of awareness you need to have. The first is to understand what the most effective teams or businesses look like and how they behave and how near your team is to emulating them. The second is to understand what it takes to lead such a team. Do you personally have the necessary attributes for success and where should your focus be in order to improve?

Team assessment

Use the following checklist to assess the current state of your team or business, considering each element in turn. Use a simple red–amber–green evaulation system.

→ Red highlights areas where you disagree strongly with the statement and can identify significant issues requiring immediate attention.

→ Amber suggests areas of concern and risk. Use amber where you need to do some digging to find out the right answer to the question and for categories that give you some concern but may not require immediate attention.

→ Green indicates that you are satisfied with the current state of things. Remember to review this again in 6 or 12 months as you may find that, as standards improve in all the other areas, these ones then look relatively weak!

ID	CATEGORY	EVALUATION CRITERIA	STATUS
	Management		RAG
M1	Leadership	All managers accept and understand that good management capability is critical to business success. The Board sponsors good management technique and it feeds into day-to-day activities throughout the organisation.	
M2	Understanding the business	Most people in the organisation exhibit a clear understanding of why the business exists and what its drivers and key processes are.	
M3	Strategic execution	There is a focus on a small number of high-priority strategic initiatives, which are planned and implemented well. Their progress is monitored and people act on the results.	
M4	Visibility and control	The performance of every part of the business is monitored through clearly defined indicators relating to its processes and the customers. There are targets and reports that are monitored, reviewed and reacted to.	
M5	Critical thinking skills	Managers and staff are able and encouraged to resolve problems and respond to opportunities in a structured way. Processes and systems enable this.	
M6	Management of performance	Managers know how to set clear objectives, monitor performance, reward good performance and challenge poor performance among their staff. Staff are well motivated as a result.	
M7	Development of others	There is a culture of developing people in the organisation. People adhere to formal structures for assessing performance, planning succession and addressing development needs. Coaching and mentoring are part of day-to-day managing.	
M8	Continuous improvement	As well as leading step-change initiatives, managers oversee incremental performance improvements, stopping to learn from problems or mistakes and implementing small changes as necessary.	
M10	Self-development	Managers devote time to their own development and encourage their teams to do the same.	

Having identified where the gaps are in your business or team's capabilities, let's look now at how effective you are as a manager and where you should be focusing your self-development.

Self-assessment

This section presents a self-assessment checklist of the factors that make a successful Fast Track manager. These reflect the knowledge, competencies, attitudes and behaviours required to get to the top, irrespective of your current level of seniority. Take control of your career, behave professionally and reflect on your personal vision for the next five years. This creates a framework for action throughout the rest of the book.

Use this checklist to identify where you personally need to gain knowledge or skills. Fill it in honestly and then get someone who knows you well – your boss or a key member of your team – to go over it with you. Be willing to change your assessment if people give you insights into yourself that you had not taken into account.

Use the following scoring process:

0 A totally new area of knowledge or skills

1 You are aware of the area but have low knowledge and/or lack skills

2 An area where you are reasonably competent and working on improvement

3 An area where you have a satisfactory level of knowledge and skills

4 You are consistently well above average

5 You are recognised as a key figure in this area of knowledge and skills throughout the business.

Now, reflect on the lowest scores and identify those areas that are critical to success. Flag these as status Red, requiring immediate attention. Then identify those areas that you are concerned about and flag those as status Amber, implying areas of development that need to be monitored closely. Status Green implies that you are satisfied with the current state.

ID	CATEGORY	EVALUATION CRITERIA	SCORE	STATUS
Knowledge			0–5	RAG
K1	Business drivers	You know where the organisation is heading from your understanding of the business strategy, key performance indicators and critical business processes.		
K2	Customers and competitors	You know your major customers (internal or external) and their must-haves and wants. You also have an understanding of who the best competitors are and what they do.		
K3	Stakeholders	You have identified your key stakeholders. Depending on your level, these may be shareholders, senior managers, resource providers or other teams in the organisation.		
K4	Business processes	You are clear about the critical business processes driving this organisation (for example, new product development or customer support). You understand the processes and procedures for getting things done.		
Competencies				
C1	Strategic	You can set a vision, develop a strategic plan and demonstrate the focus and tenacity required to achieve the vision.		
C2	Communication	You are a capable and persuasive communicator with your own team and with peers and senior managers. You are able to question incisively and listen.		
C3	Project management	You have the ability to define, plan, monitor and control projects. You manage change activities and initiatives in order to deliver identified performance improvements on time and within budget.		
C4	Risk management	You think ahead. You consider all aspects of your operations regularly to identify and reduce risks to the business.		

ID	CATEGORY	EVALUATION CRITERIA	SCORE	STATUS
Attitudes			0–5	RAG
A1	Positive approach	You have a belief that you can make a difference and get things done and you can transmit this to the team members so that they build from your confidence.		
A2	Problem-solving	You deal with issues as they arise rather than putting them off. You tackle problems, opportunities and decisions in a structured way.		
A3	Developing others	You understand the value to you and the business overall of developing people in your team. You use development to motivate your team.		
A4	Visionary	You can think beyond what is currently achievable to set challenging and aspirational goals for your team. You are proactive, making things happen rather than responding to events.		
Behaviours				
B1	Driving	You are prepared to see things through. No project goes according to plan, but you are not put off by early setbacks or problems – you have resilience.		
B2	Directing	You lead from the front when the situation demands. You make the team members accountable for their commitments. You are decisive when required.		
B3	Coaching	You are enthusiastic in coaching and mentoring others who have ideas or are involved in the implementation of ideas. You look for ways in which you can be the catalyst for the team.		
B4	Inclusive	You include the team (and potentially others in the organisation) in your decision-making. You generate buy-in and delegate clearly and effectively.		

Using results of the assessments

Having identified the key opportunities for development of both you and your team, devote some time to planning how you can overcome the issues raised. For deficiencies that you have found regarding your team, there may be several options for improving things.

1 **Training and development.** Seek the advice of the HR department or do your own research to identify some skill development programmes that will help your team. For example, if members of the team are not good at managing performance and disinclined to confront poor performance, they may benefit from a simple workshop to learn about giving effective feedback and objective performance management.

2 **Coaching and mentoring.** You or your peers may have considerable expertise and experience in some elements of management and are therefore well qualified to help individuals in your team who are struggling. For example, if you find that a number of your team can't grasp the concept of 'visibility and control', you should dedicate some time to working through their processes with them and guide them on the best approach to take control of their aspects of the business.

3 **Encouraging self-development.** Of course, some of your staff could well show an inclination to developing their own skills by reading, research or analysing the problem more fully. If, for instance, some of them don't have a clear understanding of how the business functions (often the case when you're working hard at the coalface in a specific part of the organisation), give them the time and encouragement needed to find out how the business ticks.

These approaches will also apply to your own development, as you work to balance out your own capabilities as highlighted by your self-assessment.

It is important not to get depressed about the output of the audits if you find the scores are low. You may find that others in the organisation are not as critical as you and, of course, all those things you currently see as problems are, in fact, opportunities for you to develop you or the team to make significant performance improvements as you go forward. That is also what is expected of you by those above.

STOP – THINK – ACT
At the end of the team and self-assessments, take time to reflect on your profile in order to do the following.

1 Identify any 'quick wins' you could achieve today.

2 See which chapters in this book could help the most. Look for areas where you could get a 'quick win' and improve matters in the short term. Ask yourself and the team these questions.

What should we do?	What will you change today, and what difference will it make (why)? How will we know if it has been successful?
Who do we need to involve?	Who else needs to be involved to make it work and why?
What resources will we require?	What information, facilities, materials, equipment or budget will be required and are they available?
What is the timing?	When will this change be implemented – is there a deadline?

Visit **www.Fast-Track-Me.com** to use the Fast Track online planning tool.

Best-in-class stakeholder advocacy development

Dr Peter Verdegem Danone Medical Nutrition

Dr Peter Verdegem Danone Medical Nutrition

In most companies and organisations, the group of external people that gets most attention from management, marketing and other functions is the customer group. Rightfully so – customers are the external relations that bring in the revenue. They are the ones who need to be convinced that the product is worthwhile their spending money on. Without them, the company cannot survive. Having said this, another maybe even more important group of people is largely overlooked, or at least not taken care of in a remotely similar way to the customers: the **stakeholders**.

Stakeholders can make or break your company. If a stakeholder group with considerable power is not served in the right way, forget about customers – your product will never reach their hands.

What is a stakeholder? Scanning through the chronological list of about 55 definitions of the term 'stakeholder' collected by Friedman and Miles in *Stakeholders, Theory and Practice*,[1] one of the best and most comprehensive books on stakeholder management, they range from 'Those groups without whose support the organisation would cease to exist'[2] to 'A person or entity that can affect, or is affected by the accomplishment of the goals of the organisation'[3].

This list of definitions provides an interesting insight into the changing and professionalising vision of the importance of stakeholders to the success of individual projects or the company as a whole. Whereas originally stakeholders were seen as a group of people that almost formed a threat to the company if their needs are not satisfied, as in the first definition, the second definition moves to seeing the stakeholder as being less company-centric and more a true business partner, someone whose needs have to be addressed in a mutually beneficial way.

Given the increasingly recognised importance of stakeholders, it is surprising that organisations are generally not structured professionally to manage their relationships with them. Typically, companies do not have a formal database of stakeholders. Even if such a list is maintained, it is usually spread out on the laptops of many individuals, is not complete, not up to date and subrelevant. The interactions with stakeholders are not managed in a professional way, but by many individuals who sometimes talk to the same stakeholders with different messages. Stakeholder relationships are often seen as being owned by individuals. Some employees even see them as a way to safeguard their position in a company – that if they were ever fired, the company would fire the stakeholder as well. Very seldom, a proactive plan is formulated for engagements with stakeholders, but interactions are usually performed ad hoc – that is, when a particular issue has arisen. Furthermore, transparency in stakeholder interactions is often absent as few in the company know that the interactions are taking place or the results of them. Finally, effective sharing and teaching of stakeholder advocacy development is typically not performed.

With all these hurdles in place, it is not surprising that most companies are not able to define and implement a coherent, proactive and transparent stakeholder advocacy development process.

[1] Friedman, A. L. and Miles, S. (2005) *Stakeholders, Theory and Practice*. Oxford: Oxford University Press.
[2] Internal memo, Stanford Research Institute, 1963.
[3] Freedmand, R. E. (1984) *Strategic Management: A stakeholder approach*. Boston, MA: Pitman.

Best-in-class stakeholder advocacy development consists of several distinct steps.

1 *Objective* analysis of the stakeholder environment. Who is, or could be, playing a role in the success of my project? Where do they work and how are they interconnected? It is necessary to understand the complete stakeholder map, as seeing the stakeholders in isolation may seriously hamper the effectiveness of future engagements with them. It is important to understand and appreciate that stakeholders operate in a multidirectional forcefield of opinions and interests, as defined by the networks of those stakeholders. If you are aiming to shape the opinion of a certain stakeholder, influencing the key actors in the stakeholder's network may be just as important as influencing that stakeholder.

2 Evaluation of the *ability* (or power) of stakeholders to influence the success of your project, as well as their *willingness* to do so. Are the stakeholders particularly powerful in influencing the success of your project because they are members of a decision-making body or are they merely sideways connected to your project? Do the stakeholders have a particular agenda they are trying to accomplish, either helping your cause or acting against it? It is important to consider that the evaluation of the importance of stakeholders is often biased by the personal history that the team members have with them. Meaningful evaluation can therefore be performed by holding a team session in which the importance of stakeholders is discussed and challenged.

3 *Objective* prioritisation of the engagements that are being planned with the individual stakeholders. The priority of interactions needs to be set, based on the ability and willingness of the stakeholders to influence your project. Powerful stakeholders that also have a high willingness to act are the first ones to keep track of and prepare an action plan for. Stakeholders with other combinations of *ability* and *willingness* may be dealt with a little later.

4 *Proactive* formulation of a communication strategy towards the individual stakeholders. Actions should be planned beforehand, not on an ad hoc basis when an issue has arisen. People in organisations are typically full of plans, but lacking in execution of those plans – mostly because of poor planning. Usually this results in stakeholders being approached too late or in an inconsistent way, leaving the impression that they are only being contacted if something is needed from them.

EXPERT VOICE

5 Perform consistent and appropriate *follow-up*. When promises are made, stick to them. If stakeholders ask for something, try to deliver it. Treat stakeholders as your true partners and friends – often a simple catch-up phone call or drink in the bar may be the most effective engagement.

6 Assure *transparent* documentation of the interactions that have occurred. For those of us who have worked in large organisations and developed external relationships, we all recognise the frustration of discovering that a colleague has been speaking to 'your' stakeholder. If that person has tried to push a different agenda with the stakeholder, it is often even more frustrating. Also, from the stakeholder's point of view, being contacted by several people from the same organisation with different messages is confusing and does not help to establish the credibility and professionalism of your organisation. Another reason for consistent documentation is to reduce the business risk associated with staff turnover. If people are leaving the company, the stakeholder relationships built by these people may leave as well.

7 *Evaluation* of the results of stakeholder interactions. Evaluation and analysis is essential to constantly improve stakeholder engagements and allows the transfer of best practices across the company. Consider giving an award or special recognition for a great example of stakeholder advocacy development, to motivate learning from each other and assure continued organisational improvement. Sharing best practices is often difficult because the perceived return on investment of that activity from the viewpoint of the person sharing the best practice is low as there is no immediate pay-off to picking up the phone and discussing it with another person in the company. Switching from *sharing* best practice to *acquiring* best practice is powerful. The return on investment of acquiring a best practice is much higher as the individual doing so directly benefits from this action. One way to do this effectively is to establish an internal communications position or use software solutions that allow smart cross-searching in project management systems.

By implementing these seemingly obvious steps in your organisation, you will be starting to see stakeholders not as hurdles along your path but partners on the road to success.

PART B

BUSINESS
FAST TRACK

I rrespective of your chosen function or discipline, look around at the successful managers who you know and admire. We call these people Fast Track managers, people who have the knowledge and skills to perform well and fast track their careers. Notice how they excel at three things:

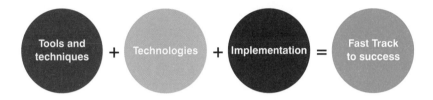

Tools and techniques

They have a good understanding of best practices for their particular field. This is in the form of methods and techniques that translate knowledge into decisions, insights and actions. They understand what the best companies do and have an ability to interpret what is relevant for their own businesses. The processes they use are generally simple to explain and form a logical step-by-step approach to solving a problem or capturing data and insights. They also encourage creativity – Fast Track managers do not follow a process slavishly where they know they are filling in the boxes rather than looking for insights on how to improve performance. This combination of method and creativity produces the optimum solutions.

They also have a clear understanding of what is important to know and what is simply noise. They either know this information or have it at their fingertips as and when they require it. They also have effective filtering mechanisms so that they don't get overloaded with extraneous information. The level of detail required varies dramatically from one situation to another – the small entrepreneur will work a lot more on the knowledge they have and in gaining facts from quick conversations with experts, whereas a large corporate may employ teams of analysts and research companies. Frequently when a team is going through any process they uncover the need for further data.

Technologies

However, having the facts and understanding best practice will achieve little unless they are built into the systems that people use on a day-to-day basis. Fast Track managers are good at assessing the relevance of new information technologies and adopting the appropriate ones in order to maximise both effectiveness and efficiency.

Implementation

Finally, having designed the framework that is appropriate to them and their team, Fast Track managers have strong influencing skills and are also great at leading the implementation effort, putting in place the changes necessary to build and sustain the performance of the team.

How tightly or loosely you will use the various tools and techniques presented in Part B will vary, and will to a certain extent depend on personal style. As you read through the following three chapters, first seek to understand how each could impact you and your team, and then decide what level of change may be appropriate given your starting point, authority and career aspirations.

FAST TRACK TOP TEN

A top golfer has a whole host of attributes – a great swing, good caddie, sure touch around the greens, deadly putting, ambition, an inspirational coach, confidence and vision. To excel in each of these areas requires real dedication and conviction. Consistently great golfers recognise the different facets of the game and systematically develop each area to create an irresistible momentum of success. Success is rarely about luck. It can be about natural talent, but, in most cases, it is about identifying exactly what to do and when to do it.

This chapter presents a framework of methods or techniques to improve performance and help you develop your irresistible momentum of success. Each function can take a lifetime to master, but the Fast Track manager will know which areas to focus on – get those areas right and the team will perform. Often success relates to the introduction of simple tools and techniques to improve effectiveness and efficiency.

Introducing management tools and techniques

As a manager, you will be on a lifelong journey, seeking to drive your career through the intelligent management of your working environment. When thinking of the top ten building blocks for successful management given below, it is worth considering them as part of a simple journey, working through strategic tools, people and delivery.

Strategic tools will set your overall strategy and direction and provide a backdrop against which you will perform and measure your success. You cannot start on a journey without determining your destination.

1 **Knowing your business** helps you understand the mechanics and drivers of your organisation. This in turn serves as a basis for determining your strategic value within the business.

2 **Setting out a vision** articulates your vision, sets a strategy and identifies long-term objectives for a business.

People. Your success will depend largely on you, but also how you interact with others. It could be a lonely and dangerous journey without good, supportive travelling companions.

3 **Being the manager you need to be** is a good starting point. Improve your personal performance by building self-awareness, managing your development and getting useful feedback.

4 **Developing individuals** builds the performance of those around you by means of the techniques of coaching, mentoring and monitoring and managing performance.

5 **Building teams** to accelerate the delivery of your goals requires analysis skills and techniques for bringing people together. It also depends on an ability to manage delegation.

6 **Building advocacy** in a fast-moving world that is becoming hierarchically less well-defined maintains the support of key stakeholders, which is vital if you are to succeed.

Delivery. To realise your goals and ambitions, you and your team must actually make the journey. To do this you must map the route, measure your progress and manage the problems that arise along the way.

7 **Changing direction** addresses the approaches you can take to steer the business or your team towards your long-term goals. These include the use of project management and aligning people in terms of values and commitment.

8 **Driving excellence** builds incremental performance improvements in your daily operations and business processes.

9 **Visibility and control** measures your progress, homing in on the key numbers and having the tools and techniques to use the numbers.

10 **Taking control** gives you tools for managing meetings, making decisions, dealing with issues and risks.

You will have noticed, after a quick glance at the Fast Track top ten, that some of these approaches may extend beyond what you would normally regard as 'management'. That is because the manager's role is changing. Senior managers are no longer excited by implementers and process followers; they now expect enterprise from their team members and want leaders at all levels in the business to deliver quantum leaps in performance. The tools and techniques you will read about in this book are designed to give you the skills to map and achieve these quantum changes.

Now, let's look at each of the tools and techniques in more detail.

1 STRATEGIC TOOLS *Knowing your business*

The Fast Track manager knows where and how value is being added. Understanding the way in which your business works, its key drivers, processes, functions, inputs, outputs and metrics are a simple but vital means of positioning your strategy and your unique way of adding value.

In large corporations, there is always a risk that managers will see themselves – or, worse, be perceived – as just another cog in the machine. To elevate you and your strategy out of the middle-management soup, you must make sure that you are not a cog. You must understand the major strategic importance and increasing value-add associated with your forward-looking goals and strategies.

QUICK TIP *SHORT ON INSPIRATION?*
Use your SWOT analysis to develop a clear plan of the
services/value you and your function should be delivering
for your most important (existing or new) stakeholders.

The modern business organisation

Deconstructing an organisation can be seen as a daunting task, but it
must be done in order to see where and how you fit. The key is to think
of the organisation as a simple series of interconnecting blocks.

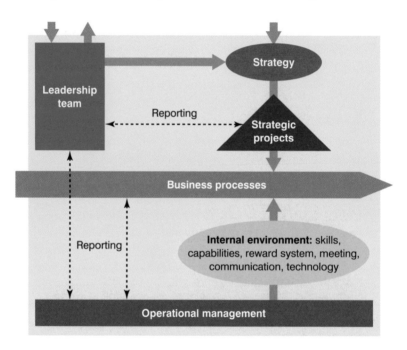

Strategy

People tend to shy away from the concept of strategy, as it is often felt
to be the domain of sophisticated and expensive management consultants. Actually, mapping your business strategy is very simple – just
answer the following questions.

→ What are the key products/services we offer to customers?

→ What are the key markets?

→ What are the key goals and drivers of the business?

→ What are its key strengths and areas of emphasis?

Look at the following examples of answers and apply the same thinking to your business.

	Airline	Premium hotel chain	Premium water supplier
Key products	Business travel	Business-class hotels	Key brands …
Key markets	Current – EU business New – Asia	Business travellers	Global – everyday water and occasions
Metrics	Seat occupancy, revenues/seat, flight turnaround time	Room occupancy, revenues/room, staff numbers/guest	Penetration, Net Sales Volume
Strengths	Brand/dual hub/ experience	Customers are ever present so can be easily targeted	Brand and vertical integration
Areas for emphasis	Grow business-class contribution Need to understand better the needs of Asian business	Increase occupancy by off-peak business Loyalty programme – make it look more generous, more family-friendly	Move more into occasions/specialised water Market segmentation and reduce volumes on discounted deals

Strategic projects

An effective business will not trust to luck in achieving its strategic goals. It will have identified and set in train a series of key initiatives and projects. Which strategic projects are you aware of? How do you fit in with or support the objectives of these projects? Will your strategy be an enabler of strategic success for the wider business?

Business process

A process differs from a project in that it is a continuously looping cycle of activity. Often, processes will be described as 'business-as-usual' (BAU). Processes are the basic building blocks of an organisation. Put simply, they are the mechanics of an organisation and the means by which organisations generate profits – or not! In most organisations, there will be HR processes, supply chain processes, sales and market- ing processes, production processes and so on. Your challenge is to recognise the processes that are impacted by your strategy and ensure that the impact is positive, maximised and lasting.

Have a look at this simple depiction of a product innovation process.

→ In identifying the value you add, think about the people involved in the process. How do you support them?

→ Some processes, such as sales or purchasing, have external interfaces. Typically, these processes will be the high-cost/high-value-generating processes – ensure, where possible, that your strategy supports these processes effectively.

Metrics

All successful businesses have clear metrics and key performance indicators (KPIs) that are used by managers to track and monitor business performance. You should identify which metrics you can contribute to directly or indirectly and how you need to set or adjust your own metrics.

Metrics can be public and high-profile, such as turnover, share price and customer satisfaction. Some metrics can be subtler and even 'unspoken' – staff satisfaction and the internal rumour mill, for example. Other metrics are more embedded within the business. These tend to be the KPIs associated with the performance of key processes, such as IT system availability, time to market for new products, market penetration, manufacturing costs or staff retention. Depending on your role, this is an area on which you may be most likely to have an impact.

Communication

All businesses must communicate information. The flow of data around strategic messages, performance requirements, metrics and organisational 'news' is key to driving performance and maintaining a sense of corporate identity. Understand your organisation's communication processes to ensure that you do not miss vital data and use the processes to convey your messages effectively.

Issue resolution

Facing a complex business scenario, how does a business deconstruct the issues and develop strategies to resolve problems and exploit opportunities? Does the business have set procedures (often seen in IT functions) or does it simply allow people to get on with it, provided there is a level of visibility around highlighting and resolving the issue?

This model helps you to understand your organisation – where and how it does business. It also acts as a framework to help pinpoint where you fit and currently add value. Most importantly, it is the springboard for the Fast Track Manager: helping to establish the key areas of value and, therefore, where you need to focus in order to have the maximum positive impact.

 CASE STORY *BEHAVIOUR AND VALUE, ALAIN'S STORY*

Narrator Alain had been running a successful chemical operation in France. A German organisation had acquired it. As part of the deal, Alain had been installed as head of the organisation's European marketing function.

Context Like all major players in the chemicals industry, the organisation grew or contracted in line with the local GDP in key markets. This ebb and flow was traditionally accepted as the norm, but the new owners were keen to change thinking and drive profitability.

Issue The majority of the organisation's business came from commodity sales, which had a low margin. Years of intelligent, market-focused new product development had created some unique non-commodity solutions, but taking these products to market at the right margins was proving difficult in an environment driven not by value but 'cost plus' pricing.

Solution Alain developed a simple approach (using external consulting support) to determine the value of a product in the overall production chain. Having done this, he worked on the ground with individual salespeople and target customers to explore how this value could be exploited in terms of price. The approach was rolled out on a targeted basis, with salespeople educated and equipped to work confidently with the approach. Sales managers were involved in the roll-out to ensure they kept people focused on new, high-value business (without forgetting the volume business). The KPIs were traditionally focused on volume, but they now also focused on margin and 'new product sold into an account'.

Learning Developing value-led solutions is only part of the equation; getting people to change behaviours is also key. The tool is important, but creating cross-functional buy-in is equally important. Culture and behaviours are driven by KPIs, so, to change behaviours, you need to change these KPIs. Showing your own commitment is also vital. Here, Alain didn't just develop a theory but also got his hands dirty in the field.

2 STRATEGIC TOOLS *Setting out a vision – business-as-usual and then some*

Managing yourself, your team and your function or business towards a strategic vision is an exciting prospect. Many managers never get the opportunity. Actually, scrub that. Most managers never give themselves the opportunity.

Managing performance shifts in regular operations and business-as-usual (BAU) requires good management skills if it is to be done well. To be a great manager, though, you need to be aiming for something; something that is going to get you and your team up in the morning and, when you have delivered it, is going to put you on the map. You need a vision.

Top managers set out a vision, achieve it and move on to the next challenge. It doesn't matter where they are in the organisation, they still have the right, duty and scope to develop a vision. The simple fact of the matter is, without a vision that crystallises what you are bringing to the business which is special (we call this your own value-add) and a series of aligned measurable goals, many managers are simply going through the motions – condemned to a rut of their own making.

Knowing the concrete *value* you are aiming to create will give a framework and sustainable purpose to your career. Understanding your value-add will help you build a vision that others can identify with.

So, what is value? Value is the tangible or intangible effect of your performance that materially enhances the results of your function or organisation. Value can result simply from a job well done or – on a more sophisticated level – improved processes, successfully executed projects or creating a culture that focuses on meeting the business's needs.

Value can be temporary or lasting. Winning a piece of business creates confidence that is valuable to the organisation (and, of course, revenues), but this can dissipate over time. Installing a sales excellence process that consistently and systematically drives increased revenues, however, creates a more lasting value.

Identifying the value you add

Look at the area you are managing and determine what it delivers (services and/or products) and how it works. Ask yourself how each of these could be improved. The answer will be the basis of your own value-add and the starting point for your vision.

Decision rights – creating your opportunity

Intelligent managers are not daunted by the power they have or don't have when it comes to setting out a vision and making meaningful change happen. Setting a vision and strategy shouldn't just happen in the boardroom. In the best businesses, it happens at every level and is driven through by the best managers. While it's important to take control of the decisions within your remit, be careful not to overstep the mark – that is, don't try to solve world hunger at a stroke, but, instead, aim to feed a village. Here are a couple of examples.

→ A category manager in a beverage company, launching a new product into a new channel when the rest of the business has exited that channel is taking a step too far. The manager may feel that it fits with his vision of the category, but it still needs to fit within the corporate framework. Checking your vision, goals, strategy and tactics with senior management is a wise move – you may get the go-ahead, but you may get some alternative suggestions. After all, you are exploring the boundaries of your right to make strategic decisions.

→ An HR manager wants to revise terms and conditions for employees in Sector 1 as they are not compatible with those for employees in all the other sectors. Suppose that Sector 1 is likely to be rationalised next year. Your vision of a homogenised set of terms for all employees makes sense, but it is not compatible with company strategy – or maybe it is, but not yet. Again, you are testing the boundaries of your strategic decision rights.

Look for the boldest, highest-value vision that has the most impact, then validate it in the context of the broader corporate strategy.

Setting a vision – a statement of intent

There is a degree of scepticism and world weariness about claims that 'We will be the best team offering world-class service levels and enabling the business to exploit its core strengths in key markets'. Such statements can be seen as 'motherhood and apple pie' – that is, nothing more than an easy soundbite, full of corporate aphorisms that seem to clog free thinking and entrepreneurial behaviour.

Actually, done well, such statements can and should be very powerful. So, why do they fail? Primarily, there is often little to back up the grandiose ambition expressed. What are the measures of success? What strategies and tactics do we need to put in place in order to deliver? How will we secure the buy-in of key players to support our initiatives and actions?

Successful managers have a vision, but also a deep-rooted understanding of what underpins that vision and how it will add real value to the business. On its own, the vision statement is a hostage to fortune – something that will be levelled against you if you don't deliver – but it is still the right place to start.

So, what constitutes a good vision? It needs to be specific, ambitious and stretching, but not beyond your remit. It should also be simple and the goals and measures of success that you will establish should fit neatly into it.

The HR manager of a global business could do worse than aiming for the following vision:

We will be the best HR function delivering world-class service.

As a vision, it is clear and stretching and clearly implies that to get there requires a change. It also articulates that, once achieved, there will be significant benefits to all stakeholders.

Here are some less effective visions.

We will cut costs in HR.

This doesn't address the concept of value creation and is not necessarily motivating. It may be an important deliverable in a strategy, but it is not a vision.

We will be so good that all global HR functions will be transferred to this country.

Well, it is certainly stretching, but it is also maybe a little beyond the HR manager's remit and strategic decision rights. It is also not wise to be deliberately contentious – unless you are very sure of your ground.

Often, the process of developing a vision is a powerful motivator, so it may be appropriate to involve your team. While this may take longer than your individual effort, it significantly shortens and simplifies the subsequent communication of the vision. Look in the Director's toolkit in Section D for processes for developing vision.

Goals – the tangible measure of an achieved vision

We will be the best HR function delivering world-class service.

It sounds good, but, 18 months down the track, how are you going to prove to everybody (including yourself) that you have delivered on your vision? You need goals and targets against which you can measure your progress.

→ HR will score more than a 95 per cent approval rating in the stakeholder satisfaction survey – current rating is 63 per cent.

→ Our service will be more user-friendly – for example, all personal development plans will be online.

→ We will be seen as a value-adding business partner – there will be an annual review of the development needs of each function to support their strategic aims.

→ We will be cost-neutral – all investments will be offset by means of cost–benefit analyses.

Your goals should be stretching and they should be SMART. SMART is an acronym that has become very popular with individuals wishing to set clear objectives. While many people know what the acronym stands for (or variants thereof), however, few understand what it actually means in terms of the objectives in question.

To eliminate misunderstandings, the SMART acronym is defined in the Fast Track top ten tools as:

→ Specific – separate multiple objectives and make them detailed and clear

→ Measurable – putting a measurable number on an objective makes it more specific and unequivocal, which is good if you want to give people clear targets and good if you want to measure their performance

→ Agreed – get all stakeholders to understand and agree to the objective to ensure full commitment

→ Realistic – ask yourself if there is enough time/resources (people or materials) to complete this objective and check that it is not in conflict with other activities needing your or your team's time

→ Time bound – to drive performance, all objectives should have a deadline.

QUICK TIP *BE INSPIRATIONAL*
Make sure that your vision fires people up (and not just in your team). Learn how to explain and sell your vision, briefly and enthusiastically.

CASE STORY *THE NEW JOB, HARRY'S STORY*

Narrator Harry had managed a 200-strong division of a global telecommunications provider for four years. He was successful and respected. His team had developed new ways of working that had won industry-wide recognition.

Context The company was changing – IT was being centralised according to product type and Harry's role was redundant. The company did not want lose him, so offered him a promotion to director level – not in IT, but in a global contract support role.

Issue The new role wasn't new just to Harry but also to the business. It was a new function. Harry figured that even a contracts expert would struggle, so how on Earth was he going to succeed? Several of the pre-existing local teams saw Harry's initiative as a threat to their continued existence.

Solution Harry went back to first principles: he mapped out the strategy for his role and developed a roadmap for its execution. He identified key metrics and critical success factors to help guide performance. He managed his team at arm's length, enabling its members to get on with their jobs and, at the same time, he systematically built a network of senior-level stakeholders who would benefit from the outputs of his new team. Within 18 months, Harry's team had risen from 25 to 75 people, with revenue per employee being higher than that for any other team and actual revenues up by some 400 per cent.

Learning Don't be a rabbit in the headlights. If you are given a (huge) challenge, tackle it in a systematic manner. Break it down into achievable deliverables and get your team motivated about your strategy. Never underestimate the importance of networking and senior management support. Lack of peer support will not be an obstacle if you get the right level of senior support and can develop and perform against metrics that will be relevant and interesting to senior managers.

 QUICK TIP *BE ASPIRATIONAL*
Visions that set significant challenges often achieve a stretched performance and sometimes hit the vision itself, whereas plans that build incrementally from the present situation achieve just that.

3 PEOPLE *Being the manager you need to be*

Becoming a successful manager or an inspiring leader is an exciting prospect. While some appear to be born with the gift, most of us have to learn the skills, work out how to build on our strengths and overcome our weaknesses. The good news is that the science of good management can be deconstructed and learned. The challenge is to find ways to change your behaviour to continuously be that Fast Track manager.

A good place to start is to think about perception. What we see is our truth and drives our take on the events and personalities around us. What is your perception of yourself and do you think that those around you agree? (You may already have seen a conflict in perception when your annual appraisal with your manager outlines a required skill you felt that you had or a failing you didn't perceive.)

When you know how you perceive the world and what colours your perceptions, you can start to take charge and see the world for what it is and not what you *think* it is. Let us consider an example.

A person sees all team sports as a mindless pursuit of collective thinking with no room for individual thinking. On reflection, that person realises this perception is coloured by a history of being excluded from such activities as a child – there may be an element of jealousy creeping in which leads to a biased perception. Accepting this, team sports can be viewed anew as great opportunities for people to meld together and achieve more than can be achieved as a series of individuals – oh, and it is also good exercise!

Without such self-awareness, the misconception would continue and the manager would not see the truth and opportunities or issues associated with that truth.

Know yourself

To get to know yourself better, let's look at two of the simpler tools for improving self-awareness. The first, the Insights Discovery four personality types wheel (see below), gives a clearer understanding of your preferences and how these relate to your personality and how you tend to operate. The second is feedback. We'll see more about giving feedback below, but what matters here is your attitude to *receiving* feedback.

Personality profile[1]

To get a quick guide on your behavioural preferences, go to Part D, The Director's toolkit, and find the Insights Discovery four personality types wheel. The outcome of this exercise will indicate your colour energy preference (Fiery Red, Sunshine Yellow, Earth Green or Cool Blue). Look at the strengths and weaknesses associated with your colour energies and make sure that these roughly align with your experience.

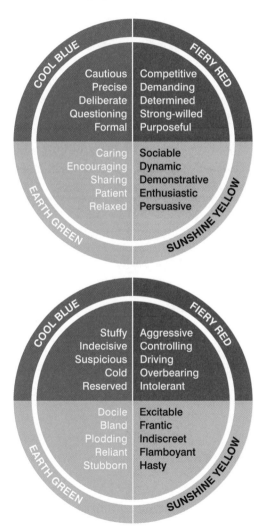

[1] © Insights Discovery.

There are two things to consider at this stage.

→ Make sure that you maximise and build on your strengths and reduce the impact of your weaknesses. For instance, if you have a preference for Fiery Red energy, you may be less inclined to involve others and bring them with you. One possible development output is for you to consciously increase the involvement of people in your decision-making. Meanwhile, your strengths will lie in leading and driving teams to task completion. If you have a preference for Earth Green energy, you may feel more concerned about the harmony of the team rather than the decision at hand. Try to separate the 'feelings' side of the decision from the rational aspects and use your diplomatic skills to get others to buy into your decision.

→ Consider your impact on others and how you can use the Insights Discovery approach to interact with others. Look at the colour energy opposite yours on the wheel. The characteristics described there may be foreign to you. Who can you think of, among your colleagues, who fits that opposite type description? Does this person frustrate or irritate you? What strategies can you develop for interacting with this person *on their terms*? For example, if you personally have high Sunshine Yellow energy, the best approach to influencing someone who you have identified as having Cool Blue energy is to give him or her a structured, reasoned argument, supported by documentation, and give the person time to make a decision.

These strengths and weaknesses exist as part of your natural make-up. You can decide to improve or circumvent what you find, but you should also derive courage and self-belief from an understanding that these are normal personality traits.

Feedback

Feedback is potentially the most powerful source of information about your performance gaps. It will only be given if you allow it to be given. 'Feedback is the breakfast of champions', said Ken Blanchard, implying that *real* self-development starts with feedback. As a manager, you should be striving to overcome any barriers your team or colleagues have to giving you feedback. Typical barriers are a negative reaction from you, such as denial, defensiveness, anger or justification, and that they are unsure how to give it (see the DESC model for giving feedback in this chapter, under 4 People: Developing individuals). Of course, the best way to get the culture of feedback going is to set the best example. Be structured, specific and non-blaming when you give feedback and follow it up with the invitation, 'What could I do differently to help you achieve your goals?'

If you're getting feedback, you may need to 'broaden your shoulders' a little because you may not enjoy the implied criticism. Remember, feedback will come from other people's perceptions. This is not necessarily right or wrong, just different and will tie in very closely with the personality differences described above. Before reacting, think about your intentions and focus on how you can use this feedback to lift your performance.

Feedback can also be made anonymous to allow people to be frank. This often takes the form of 360° feedback (from all those around you – your boss(es), peers and team). To conduct 360° feedback, have your assistant or a member of your team administer the process so that responders are assured of anonymity. Also, prepare yourself – some of the feedback may be harsher than you expect!

Develop yourself

→ **Set your personal goals.** These will be short-term, covering how you can improve in your current role, and longer-term, to cover your career planning (see Part C). Set development goals to overcome the gaps between your current ability and the skills and techniques that are required to do your current role or the next role or, indeed, those that will make you a more rounded manager. Try to keep your goals SMART and limit their number. Make sure that you can deliver on your goals, so, be ambitious, but don't set yourself too stretching a target.

→ **Map the gaps.** Using the management assessment in Chapter 2, identify where you think the most significant gaps are in your management capability. Add the top five issues from your profile and feedback – these may be weaknesses you want to overcome or strengths that are underdeveloped.

→ **Plan.** Set yourself milestone targets and plot activities to deliver on your development goals.

→ **Use mentors.** If you aspire to a certain position or level, find someone in that position to mentor you. Talk to your potential mentor about your goals and how you see him or her helping you; make it easy. Even if your mentor doesn't help much, he or she will be flattered and impressed that you asked.

→ **Use a coach.** If you struggle to keep to your own development promises, relegating them in priority when important operational stuff comes along, enlist a coach to keep you honest. You could choose a peer or your boss or, better still, someone at a greater remove, such as someone from HR or an external coach.

→ **Find skill development courses.** Identify courses and workshops that will give you the skills you need. Use your peers, HR or your network outside the company to identify useful courses. HR may well have a set of management development modules running in-house that may be relevant to your needs. If you find an external course, you may need to pay for it out of your cost centre, so make sure that this is planned into your budgets.

→ **Evaluate regularly.** Make time to review your progress against your goals and solicit feedback to confirm any progress made.

The proactive manager[2]

The Fast Track manager takes control of his or her world rather than the other way round, so it is vital that you allow time to develop a proactive rather than a reactive attitude. Reactive managers will feel too busy, stressed, short of time, powerless, unchanging and short of options. Proactive managers will feel a step ahead – anticipating, initiating, planning, taking charge and being in control.

[2] From Waldock, T. and Kelly-Rawat, S. (2004) *The 18 Challenges of Leadership*. Harlow: Prentice Hall.

The proactive challenge

Are you proactive or reactive? Take the test below to find out. Read through the questions and, in the context of your current role, give yourself a score on a scale of 1 to 10 for each pair of statements, where 10 means that you strongly agree with the statement on the left and 1 means you strongly agree with the statement on the right.

10...1		Score
You feel in control of your time	Others largely control it	
You spend your time on what is important	You spend your time on what is urgent	
You act on your concerns	You react to other people's agendas	
You lead your day	You manage your in-tray	
You say, 'I, Can, Will, What's Possible?'	You say, 'You, They, Can't, Won't, Don't know'	
You seek to influence or change something	You accept this is how it is	
You are interested in possibilities and opportunities	You are preoccupied with the problem	
You are doing what you want to be doing	You are doing what you ought to be doing	
	Total score	

The maximum potential score is 80, so, if you scored near this, you clearly regard yourself as a proactive manager. If you scored between 40 and 60, you are acknowledging that there are opportunities for more proactive behaviour. If you scored below 40, you may feel that your day is driven by your 'to do' list and other people's agendas. You probably feel that you are not making significant progress towards your goals. Use the planner below to work out how to make better use of your time and take a more proactive position regarding your work.

The key to becoming a proactive manager is to plan how you use your time. You can use the matrix below as both an assessment of your current activity and a planner for future activity. To assess your current workload, list the activities you have done in the past week.

	High urgency *(immediate deadlines)*	**Low urgency** *(long or no deadlines)*
High importance *(critical to the business or achieving strategic goals)*		
Low importance *(in relation to the business or strategic goals)*		

Here's a worked example.

Production manager, John, recorded his activity over a week, as follows.

	High urgency *(immediate deadlines)*	**Low urgency** *(long or no deadlines)*
High importance *(critical to the business or achieving strategic goals)*	→ Ran capital engineering meeting → Visited supplier with ongoing quality issues → Monitored trials on the production line → Conducted a disciplinary review	→ Started (but did not complete) training needs assessment for team → Reviewed my personal development plan
Low importance *(in relation to the business or strategic goals)*	→ Responded to emails as they came in → Produced production reports → Attended production meetings → Called round shift managers to cover for sickness → Checked overtime records	→ Completed HR attendance analysis → Looked online for potential spare parts supplier

Looking at this, John realises that he has made virtually no progress on his strategic or personal goals. So, he reviewed the chart and managed the output as follows.

	High urgency *(immediate deadlines)*	**Low urgency** *(long or no deadlines)*
High importance *(critical to the business or achieving strategic goals)*	→ Ran capital engineering meeting – **too high importance to delegate** → Visited supplier with ongoing quality issues – **delegate to quality manager** → Monitored trials on the production line – **delegate to section managers** → Conducted a disciplinary review – **retain**	→ Started (but did not complete) training needs assessment for team – **complete by end next week** → Reviewed my personal development plan – **diarise regular plant tours to meet/motivate staff** → **Set up strategic project review meetings** → **Plan for staff development and succession** → **Diarise two half days per week for strategic activity** → **Diarise strategic meetings with team**
Low importance *(in relation to the business or strategic goals)*	→ Responded to emails as they came in – **set three times in the day for emails** → Produced production reports – **delegate to section managers** → Attended production meetings – **keep doing for now** → Called round shift managers to cover for sickness – **delegate to section managers** → Checked overtime records – **delegate to section managers**	→ Completed HR attendance analysis – **delegate to assistant** → Looked online for potential spare parts supplier – **delegate to engineering manager as a new objective**

4 PEOPLE Developing individuals

The bulk of a manager's job is to get the best out of people. While there will be plenty of tasks to occupy him or her, the role is not to do but to coordinate; organise people around tasks and strategy; deal with issues that people have in the course of their work; coach, encourage and motivate; and instil the culture and attitude that will deliver the manager's strategic goals and value to the business.

Motivating people

When asked what motivates people, we often think about working conditions, salary or job status. In his revolutionary work, however, Frederick Herzberg identified these as 'hygiene factors' – elements that will demotivate or upset people if they are not in place.

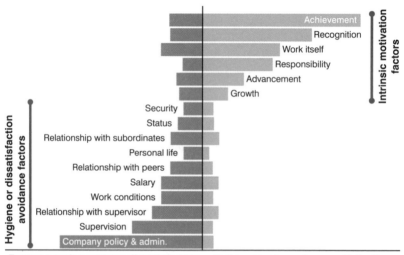

Factors causing extreme dissatisfaction   Factors causing extreme satisfaction

ADAPTED FROM HERZBERG, F. (2003) 'ONE MORE TIME: HOW DO YOU MOTIVATE EMPLOYEES?', *HARVARD BUSINESS REVIEW* (JANUARY), PP. 87–96. REPRODUCED BY PERMISSION.

Herzberg's research proved that people will strive to meet these hygiene needs because they are unhappy without them. Once the hygiene factors have been satisfied, the effect soon wears off – satisfaction is temporary. Poorly managed organisations fail to understand that people are not motivated by their hygiene needs being addressed. People are only truly motivated when they are enabled to reach for and satisfy the factors that Herzberg identified as the real motivators.

When you want to motivate your team, therefore, make sure that you have satisfied the motivation factors. Do they know the following?

→ What's expected of them

→ How this fits in with the big picture

→ What resources and support they can rely on

→ How they'll be measured

→ How they'll be rewarded for success

→ How they're valued

→ How they're doing.

Assessing the team and succession planning

Before thinking about development needs, think first about how you rate the people in your team. Could they at some point be promoted to a more senior role, your role or perhaps further up the organisation?

Succession planning is worth doing at most levels in an organisation. It motivates your team members to know that you are thinking about their progress and development and it sends a clear signal to those above you that you are building the human capital of the business.

Next, think about the possible moves for each person in your team. Some might benefit from a move into a peer's role to increase their experience; others may be identifiable as potentially taking your role or one of your peers' roles.

Uncovering development needs

Development needs can be uncovered by your own objective judgement of individuals, backed up by views from their teams and your peers. The most powerful commitment to development comes, however, when individuals identify their own needs. If you or they have an idea of their next move, use the job description for the new role to benchmark their current performance and identify any gaps.

Remember that some types of development (particularly training) will require a spend of some kind. This may be housed in HR's budget or you may have to pay for it yourself from your own department's budget. In which case, make sure that you have the training needs for your team built in when you go through the annual budgeting process.

Types of development

Training

This is one of the most popular forms of development. It can take many forms, from MBAs and leadership development through to specific job skill courses. It can be 'hard', such as project management, or 'soft' – influencing skills, for example. There isn't space here to deal with the range of options, but it is worth thinking about the benefits to you and your team.

On the plus side, training will be motivating, open people's minds to new ideas and provide useful tools and techniques. Don't see training as a stand-alone performance changer – work with any individuals to ensure that they come back to work with a clear agenda for change and support this by conducting regular reviews and coaching.

Feedback

This is a very powerful tool for identifying performance gaps and stimulating effort to change. Feedback can be positive and constructive. Being positive is not difficult, but we rarely do enough of it, so it's important to build it into conversations with your team. The latter, being constructive, is more challenging as you may be worried about upsetting the other person. Alternatively, you may be bold and blunt and end up with a defensive culture in the office.

You can find tips on receiving feedback under 3 People: Being the manager you need to be, earlier in this chapter, but here's a simple tool for giving feedback in such a way that the message is not lost in the noise of emotion and differing perceptions. It is called the DESC model.

→ **Describe.**   Describe the behaviour/situation as completely and objectively as possible. Just the facts! For example:

The monthly report you produced for the board meeting had insufficient details about your team's account development activity.

→ **Express.**   Express your feelings and thoughts about the situation/behaviour. Try to phrase your statements using 'I', not 'You'. Beginning sentences with 'You' often puts people on the defensive, which means they won't listen to you. For example:

As a result, I felt insufficiently prepared to answer questions and give an accurate account of your team's activity.

→ **Specify.** Specify what behaviour/outcome you would prefer to happen. For example:

> *In future, I would like to see detailed account development plans for your team's top ten clients included in every monthly report.*

→ **Consequences.** Specify the consequences (both positive and negative). Here are some examples:

> *If you can do this every month, then not only will the Board get a more accurate account of what's going on but it will also reflect your commitment to increasing the team's activity levels.*

> *If you don't provide more detailed activity reports, the Board may lose confidence in your ability to manage your team effectively.*

> *Providing me with a more detailed report gives me more confidence to stand up in front of the other Board members and discuss your team's activities.*

Here are a few tips for giving effective feedback:

→ make sure that it is frequent and timely – make it part of 'how we work' and immediate

→ ensure that it is relevant and noise-free – that is, not tinged with an emotional charge

→ it should be specific and accurate, so say, for example, 'Please underline your titles in future' rather than 'Your report was rubbish'

→ the receivers should always confirm that they understand the nature of the feedback and accept that it is something they should work on.

Mentoring

This can make a significant difference to people's performance, as you will know if you have ever had a boss who showed you how to do something, encouraged you to practise and praised you as you made progress. Mentoring is an excellent way to pass on skills that may be job-specific, or more general management skills that you have identified as development needs. Make sure that you give your mentoring programme some structure and goals. The real challenge for the mentor in a busy world is to keep it to the forefront. Like coaching, mentoring requires a proactive approach and should be diarised in the Low urgency/High importance box in the matrix on page 56.

Coaching

Coaching is increasingly seen as the most powerful of the development tools, as this technique delivers results by raising awareness and generating responsibility. The key difference between coaching and mentoring is that coaches enable their coachees to analyse problems themselves, identify their own solutions and take ownership and responsibility for changes. A coach does this by challenging, questioning and encouraging, as well as by means of a process: the GROW model.[3]

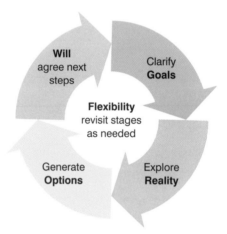

The GROW model involves four stages:

1 **Goal** Clarify with the coachee what topic he or she would like to cover in this meeting and agree on a goal and outcome: 'What are we going to cover in this session? What would success look like at the end of this meeting?' Build rapport and put the coachee at ease, create openness, be engaged and responsive.

2 **Reality** Establish the current situation as accurately as possible: 'What is happening now? What have you done about it

[3] Whitmore, J. (1992) *Coaching for Performance*. London: Nicholas Brealey.

so far? How would you rate it on a scale of 1 to 10?' Ask open questions, listen and explore by gentle probing.

3 **Options** List all the possible options. Don't draw up an action plan at this stage. Encourage the learner to think of different ways of dealing with the issue or problem: 'What options do you have? What else? What might others do?'

4 **Will** Develop an action plan that the learner is happy to commit to. The plan must be clear, have an agreed time frame, with actions that can be achieved. Offer support and any help that might be required: 'What actions are you going to take? When are you going to do it? What barriers might you face? What review process shall we use?' In the process, give encouragement and summarise what has been agreed.

5 PEOPLE Building teams

Teams come in all shapes and sizes and, before thinking about building your team, it is worth thinking about the differing types of teamwork.

→ **Independent teams** operate as a unit – no one person can deliver a meaningful task without working with other team members. This means that individual tasks are often specialised and success is only achieved when the team works together. In sport terms, this might be a football team; in business terms, this will be a multifunctional unit, such as a management team, or business process unit, such as a manufacturing cell. Independent teams benefit from activities designed to improve the 'process' they are trying to deliver.

→ **Interdependent teams** are formed of people who do the same activity. One person can win and make the team win without influencing any other player. A singles tennis or golf team is a good sporting analogy. In a business, this could be a sales team or a call centre team. Everyone is doing much the same task and their individual performances have no direct impact on each other's performances. An interdependent team benefits from mutual support and encouragement, which can be built by engaging in social activities and getting to know each other by tackling artificial challenges.

→ **Project teams** come together for a limited period of time to solve a particular problem or deliver an objective.

→ **Virtual teams** are groups of people who communicate via a technology, be it telephone or collaborative software. Virtual team members may never physically meet.

→ In **self-managed teams**, responsibility and authority are delegated to the team, its members making decisions by consensus, voting or intimidation. Such team don't usually operate effectively without some senior management involvement or support.

Ultimately, the type of teamwork you need in your environment will be dictated by the needs of your function or organisation and the nature of the work people undertake. The Fast Track manager achieves the best or even synergistic (that is, greater than the sum of individual contributions) performance with a group of people.

Some teams seem to work well; others can struggle, perhaps because of the personalities involved, the nature of the team and so on. Here are two simple tools for analysing your team dynamics if you suspect that it could be working better.

→ **Stages of team development** Bruce Tuckman's[4] model is based on the observation that there are four (now very well-known) stages of team development.

→ **Forming** in which the team meets and learns about the opportunity and challenges, then agrees on goals and begins to tackle the tasks. Team members are usually on their best behaviour but very focused on themselves, and supervisors of the team tend to need to be in directive mode during this phase.

→ **Storming** sees the team get into the meat of the issue and team members open up to each other and confront each

[4] Tuckman, B. (1965) 'Developmental sequence in small groups', *Psychological Bulletin*, 63 (6) pp. 384–99.

other's ideas and perspectives. Supervisors still need to be in directive mode during this phase.

→ **Norming** occurs when team members adjust their behaviour to each other as they develop work habits that make teamwork seem more natural and fluid. During this phase, team members begin to trust each other, but can lose their creativity if healthy dissent is stifled.

→ **Performing**, which is when team members have become interdependent. By this time they are motivated and knowledgeable. The team members are now competent, autonomous and able to handle the decision-making process without supervision.

→ **Team roles** Meredith Belbin[5] recognised that performing teams are composed of different personalities, each of whom brings value to the team. If you think that your team has too many drivers and not enough finishers or seems to be getting nowhere because everyone is too friendly, look at the balance of the team using the Insights Discovery techniques on page 51 and work with the team to redress any imbalance.

Building your team may be important if you are facing new challenges or you require it to step up a level and deliver increased performance. Teambuilding can happen as a result of the nature of the work being undertaken. For example, new project teams will sometimes go through the phases of team development described above quite naturally. Other times, when facing tough challenges, immature teams can get stuck in the storming phase and not have great productivity.

Teambuilding exercises consist of a variety of tasks designed to develop group members and their ability to work together effectively. There are many types of teambuilding activities that range from kids' games to ones that involve novel complex tasks and are designed for specific needs. There are also more complex teambuilding exercises that are composed of multiple activities, such as ropes courses, corporate drumming and exercises that last over several days.

[5] Belbin, M. (1981) *Management Teams*. London: Heinemann.

The purpose of teambuilding exercises is to assist teams in becoming cohesive units of individuals that can work together effectively to complete tasks.

6 PEOPLE Building advocacy

The key to managerial success, it is often said, is to be found in the art of winning friends and influencing people. Just because it is a cliché doesn't devalue its currency. The successful manager recognises that he or she will achieve most when the team offers maximum support. Support from the team includes support from key stakeholders elsewhere in the environment as well. We call this **building advocacy** – establishing a body of people at all levels who will actively or passively support your vision, objectives, strategies and tactics.

A Fast Track manager builds advocacy because he or she needs:

→ committed people to do good quality work

→ senior management support to gain the commitment of the team and other colleagues – if the CEO is seen to be a supporter, then the commitment of others will be that much easier to secure.

Building advocacy as a means of securing support is clearly one way to reinforce the delivery of your strategy. The alternative is tyranny! You can either bring people with you or impose your will on people and the organisation. With respect to the commitment of budding tyrants and despots – people who are prepared to strong-arm, cajole and bully their way to success – the Fast Track manager will recognise that, while an occasional show of strength will reinforce his or her credentials as a no-nonsense, results-orientated professional, this cannot be sustained for the long haul. Tyranny is hard work and those who live by the sword die by the sword – managers who set out to achieve their goals, regardless of the impact on others, eventually will fail. Tyranny does not secure commitment. It encourages short-term behaviours directed at satisfying what may be perceived as today's targets, but it does not encourage risk-taking or intelligence.

The demise of several leading financial institutions during the economic crisis of 2008 shows how fear and tyranny can lead to short-term results that do not sustain good long-term behaviours. Quite apart from a bonus culture that drove the wrong behaviours, high-profile Credit Crunch casualties were typified by tyrannical arrogance at the highest levels. Those who dictated how people should work sought, not advocacy and commitment, but blind obedience for fear of the consequences. In the short term they got what that asked for; in the long term, some might say, they got what they deserved.

QUICK TIP *SPILL IT ALL ON THE TABLE*

When doing a SWOT, try to be open – try to think about the broader environment. Also, try to involve colleagues and trusted advisers to ensure that the SWOT is a true reflection of the issues, not just a one-dimensional reflection of your personal perspective. Once you have documented an idea, it cannot just disappear.

Controlling your stakeholders – managing human commitment to build advocacy

Tyranny   Control = **building advocacy**   **Abdication**

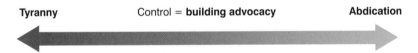

If tyranny occupies one end of a control spectrum, the other end is about casting yourself on the mercies and whims of others – abdication. There, your strategy and success will be decided by others and their perception of its validity in the context of their goals. If your strategy is right for them and they recognise this, you may be lucky and get the right results, but, by not managing the stakeholder environment, you are making yourself a hostage to fortune. If your key stakeholder is busy (highly likely) and has other people baying for his or her time, attention and resources, chances are your strategy will be drowned out. Worse still, it (and therefore you) could be seen as a distraction and a drain on resources.

Building advocacy is about occupying the middle ground. It is about having your own firm opinions and strategies and selling them to the people who matter. You will not be a tyrannical bulldozer or a laissez-faire strategist. Rather, building advocacy is about securing long-term, sustainable results that support the strategic health of the business and are aligned with the genuine needs of individuals. Building advocacy sells itself not on blinkered short-termism nor by being overly reliant on the goodwill of others, but by creating a coalition that has bought into the validity, intelligence and achievability of your goals.

To secure advocacy, the key step is to align your aims with those of your stakeholders (the key players in your business). Your advocates will support a project or an initiative for a number of reasons. To help work out what those reasons are, it is useful to understand the basic drivers of people in the workplace – why people actually come to work.

→ **The bill payer.** The key reason this person comes to work is from economic necessity – to pay the bills. Typically, the bill payer is not trying to make a name for him- or herself and often is not too bothered about being stretched or working overly hard.

→ **The social worker.** This person enjoys work primarily because it is where he or she meets friends and is a fun place to be.

→ **The intellectual.** This person is one of life's problemsolvers – work and the challenges it represents are a never-ending Sudoku game.

→ **The money maker.** This person is driven by wanting to have a career, status and money. For the money maker, work is interesting in that it enables progress to be made towards a series of tangible personal metrics – car, holidays and so on.

Note that there are many models for types of people. In the context of stakeholder motivation and your strategy, most people will fit into one of these groups. Some may be hard to pigeonhole and others may bridge types or migrate from one type to another. Categorising people is never easy and sometimes invalid, but, in this context – and done with due acceptance of the potential margin of error – it can be very useful. This particular model works well here as it helps you to understand the tendency of people to take risks and maybe go the extra mile to support your strategy.

Given the above, it is vital that you understand, in the context of what you wish to achieve, the role the stakeholder plays and the extent to which you can or have aligned your strategy and objectives with the needs of that individual. Apart from understanding how your goals will support stakeholders in achieving their own goals and KPIs, to secure *real* advocacy you will also understand how to pitch your project according to their broader styles and motivators.

→ **The bill payer.** Is your project safe? Make sure that you are not frightening them with unclear demands.

→ **The social worker.** Avoid asking this type of person to take on too many solo tasks as it will not motivate them. Think about teamwork and emphasise how this project will be good for the *team*. Can you make it feel 'fun'?

→ **The intellectual.** How does this strategy or project help them develop and become experts in their field?

→ **The money maker.** How will your project advance them in their career? Will it help them hit their KPIs? Will it help them exceed their bonus targets?

Knowing the human geography of your business – with its hills, mountains, swamps, deserts, the odd oasis, oceans and glaciers (it can feel that slow at times) – will enable you to chart a course for success. It is your starting point. You need senior management to support your strategy and vision, though. To secure their active commitment, indentify the key players, work out their business goals and drivers and ensure that – as far as is possible and practical – your strategy will address their needs. Make sure, at the very least, that you are not in *conflict* with their objectives.

A simple stakeholder analysis will help you to identify and track the commitment of key stakeholders to your vision. Use the following guidelines to build it quickly and effectively.

→ Ensure that you identify the **key players** – think of team members, high-profile external influencers, people who may be negative, but whose support/opposition will be key to your success.

→ Do not duck the **difficult people** – they will be hardest to manage, but, assuming their influence is high, winning them over will be the most important thing you can do.

→ Explicitly **link key deliverables** and objectives to the key stakeholders' drivers – don't try to be clever as the more tangible the link, the easier it will be to secure their meaningful support.

→ A **joint effort** – work with a trusted colleague to build the stakeholder analysis. This person will help you to identify key people/issues that need to be managed and develop appropriate stakeholder management strategies.

→ Done by you and for you, a stakeholder analysis will bring vital structure to your interactions with your colleagues. Developed together and *shared* with your *team*, the stakeholder analysis will open doors and drive your strategy forwards by fertilising and harnessing the enthusiasm and intellectual horsepower of the business.

  → **With your team** explain how your team members need to work with you to secure stakeholder support for their benefit as well as the project's.
  → **With key stakeholders** explain your project, how *they* fit in and why they are important. Ask them to validate your understanding of their commitment. This is a great technique because, as a form of flattery, it is likely to increase their buy-in to your objectives. It also helps to weed out any false assumptions that you may have had about their commitment levels.

→ **Sustain** your advocacy management programme. The main pitfall to recognise and avoid is that it is not enough to do this as a single one-off activity – securing support and sustaining commitment is a continuous process with continuous rewards.

→ Be prepared to **flex** to changing a stakeholder environment. No matter how well it has been developed and articulated, your strategy will never fit exactly the needs and drivers of key stakeholders. Do not force your strategy on people; modify and stretch your goals. Be prepared to make sacrifices in terms of timelines and the exact nature of what you expect. You *must* not compromise your strategy, but, equally, you *must* keep hearts and mind on board. Your conviction and force of character can, and occasionally should, do this, but your ability to meld to the environment is a truly valuable commodity.

→ Understand **influence**. To what extent can this person make your project fly or die? Hierarchy is often a simple way of understanding potential influence. It is also useful to consider people's track records. If they have been successful in similar areas, their influence on the way your aims are perceived will probably be high.

→ **Support of a stakeholder** is vital. Will he or she clear obstacles from your path or block you at every turn? Support is most easily understood by assessing the extent to which your goals and deliverables are aligned with a stakeholder's needs. They may be well aligned, but this may not be transparent, so while, in principle, support should be high, it may in fact be low as your objectives have not been clearly communicated and sold to your key stakeholder.

→ Clearly you want **maximum support from all stakeholders**. This is not always possible as what you're trying to do will not always be easy for others to swallow. At the very least, it is important to develop effective communication plans to avoid any negativity to your strategy from highly influential stakeholders.

Here is an example of a completed stakeholder analysis.

Stakeholder	Needs	Influence (1–10)	Support (–5 – +5)	Communication plan
Tom Yates, finance	Needs to know that launch of any new service will come in under budget and drive share price upwards	10	+4	Organise one-on-one presentation, sent in advance. Secure his support to manage other stakeholders
Ann Marshall, marketing	New product launches into AsiaPac will rely heavily on effectiveness of marketing. She will want all options available from day 1	6	+2	Develop action plan (draft)
Antonia Coplo, purchasing	Sourcing will be critical to success. She is driven by cost. We need to get our drivers on her agenda as well	7	–1	Organise meeting (get Tom Yates in to support)
Mark Foster, supply chain	As head of department, his head is on the block and he is looking for reliable delivery of a future service model	5	–2	Convince Mark that our strategy is well managed for risk and will offer better performance (with his support)

7 DELIVERY *Changing direction*

Developing a new vision will set the target for you and your team. The Fast Track manager then applies the appropriate tools and techniques to convert that vision into a working strategy and an execution plan. Executing your vision generally requires people to change what they do and how they do it. The case story below demonstrates the development of a clear strategy and set of tactics out of a compelling vision.

Vision to strategy

A SWOT analysis is an excellent starting point for developing your strategic options. An effective SWOT analysis will help you to identify the areas you and your team need to address and the challenges and issues you are going to accept and deal with.

CASE STORY *KEEP THE STRATEGY CLEAR, BOB'S STORY*

Narrator Bob was running a major player in the nascent digital broadcasting business at a time when the field was open, formats and products varied and no one had a clear lead in the market.

Context The organisation was in a battle with other digital providers to become the dominant player for digital TV services in the national subscription market.

Issue This was a very new market. No one operator had taken a lead or shown the directon it might go in and customers weren't ready or able to articulate what they wanted.

Solution Bob structured a very clear strategy for his staff.

Vision To make the service an irresistible no-brainer to all subscribers.

Strategy Meet the need of all potential subscribers.

Tactics Cater for every taste (sport, movies, food, arts, crime, history and more); offer range of choices – multiple packages; make it easy – one call/internet ordering; offer non-TV services; build an ultra-agile customer relationship management (CRM) system to anticipate and deliver what customers want; market the product as the default option.

Learning Simplified as it is, this story provides an example of the importance of a clear strategic decision-making framework. Anything that supported the strategy of 'meeting the need of any subscriber' was a valid tactic. If it didn't, it was a distraction and not to be done.

→ **Strengths.** Identify your current competitive (distinct from your competitors') or, at least, significant strengths and initiatives that have worked. Any strategy you develop must build on your strengths and these will also develop confidence in your current assets and performance.

→ **Weaknesses.** Given what the business is trying to achieve, where do you underperform and what kinds of initiatives tend to fail? Knowing your weaknesses guides your strategy and enables you to choose to rectify or mitigate them.

→ **Opportunities.** What changes do you see or predict happening in your environment that might present opportunities? When considering this for an entire organisation, it will be the external environment. If you represent a function or team, your environment will be the rest of the business.

→ **Threats.** Conversely, what changes in your environment might present future threats to your unit? What changes and external events may undermine your ability to deliver strategic value?

Action

Post SWOT, the worst-case scenario is that, after a really good, creative working session with the team, you file the SWOT away and it never sees the light of day again. What a waste of time! Even when it is 'used', the SWOT is often a conversation piece or a thought-starter – useful but potentially not harnessing the intellectual horsepower that was invested in its generation.

A SWOT should, therefore, have an 'Action' column, identifying where and how you are going to deal with the issues raised and integrate them into your strategy. This systematic, structured approach isn't just a checklist – it is a validation of the fact that what you are doing will add real value, exploiting your abilities and addressing your challenges.

Referring back to the example of a completed stakeholder analysis on page 72, below is an example of a completed SWOT with an 'Action' column.

This SWOT is the perfect vehicle for kick starting a focused delivery of strategy.

QUICK TIP *DIVIDE AND CONQUER*
Make sure that you use the structure of the SWOT effectively. The point of a SWOT is to enable you to break down a complex business environment into a series of discreet issues, rendering them more manageable. Within each box of the SWOT, remember not to mix issues. For example, in the SWOT below, under Threats, service and cost have been kept separate, not lumped together under the heading of competition. By doing this, each one can be targeted as required and, therefore, actions will be more effective.

SWOT for expanding supply chain activities into AsiaPac

		Action
Strengths	We have a strong team in Europe that knows our business culture We have good relationships with global clients who will work with us on this We have successfully extended our supply chain into Latin America New system is working very well with just-in-time (JIT) delivery from Europe to North America	Make sure that, with expansion, new people are introduced to that culture Take care not to let UK people appear to be telling AsiaPac what to do Make contact with the people who did the Latin America project and learn from their experiences Emphasise this to account managers and customers in AsiaPac as a unique selling proposition
Weaknesses	We have little senior management experience of AsiaPac operations We have no local language capability at HQ The team dealing with the main AsiaPac product line is new The seasonal nature of AsiaPac doesn't fit with our Europe/North America model KPIs are not clear for new supply chain activity	Look for a senior management sponsor who will help to remove this weakness by using consultants or bringing someone in with experience (and languages?)
Opportunities	This is a complex service. Our track record will be critical to success and already places us ahead of the competition Performing well here will secure future of global supply chain function We can set KPIs and possibly drive them to EMEA level? We can develop local partners who fit our needs/ways of working	Benchmark local performance – set our targets accordingly Can Latin America team help? Create a specification of ideal partner
Threats	Failure to perform will affect business revenues. Currently this project is high-profile and being watched by external analysts and shareholders The business may decide to outsource this activity to local supply chain function Competition are likely to exploit any shortfall in our service levels Competition are already able to undercut our prices	Map clear strategy/action plan Ensure that targets are realistic and measure performance regularly. Contingency plans needed for poor performance Ensure project has effective cost base – if not, review outsourcing options

This is a summary of a business plan arising out of the SWOT. To generate this, focus on vision, strategy and tactics – key areas of value-add.

GOAL *EXPANDING SUPPLY CHAIN ACTIVITIES INTO ASIAPAC*

Vision To create a reliable and effective supply chain in AsiaPac that is seen as a competitive strength.

Strategy We must be driven by speed, reliability and flexibility.

Tactics **Flexible repeatability** Ensure core range features can be repeated quickly or are easily modifiable to all needs.

Offer best-in-class tracking for internal and external stakeholders.

Design, test, do – zero ad hoc service design.

Create fast-track SC model to enable service design and approval with no bureaucracy.

What's in and what's out? Creating a strategy to match your vision
Identify the strategic decision-making framework that will guide you to your vision.

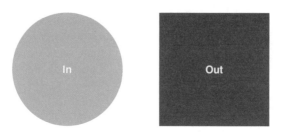

The circle represents your vision. What fits in the circle supports your vision and is core to your strategy. If an action, project or initiative doesn't fit in the circle, you have to question if it will be done. Certainly, it cannot be a priority.

Look at your function and management area. Thinking of the strategic objectives of the business, ask yourself these questions.

→ Where do I fit? What is expected of us?

→ How do we deliver currently?

→ What needs to change?

→ What should my function look like?

QUICK TIP *ESTABLISH FOCUS*
Work out what really matters to you and your strategy and
test all critical decisions and actions as to how they will
support your focus.

Strategy to tactics

*If CEOs stumble it's because of one simple shortcoming ... 70% of
the time it's bad execution. The organisation not getting things done,
being indecisive, not delivering on commitments. (Fortune)*

Many strategies are condemned to sit on the shelf – never likely to make
a recognisable impact on the business.

The cardinal sin of strategic thinking is to fail to address the question, 'What do we actually need to do to deliver the vision?' This is often
caused by the fact that the vision has never been deconstructed into
goals and strategies.

Military exploits often give us good insights into strategy and tactics
and an example from the American Civil War is particularly helpful in this
case. Towards the end of the American Civil War, it had become clear
that the South was a spent force and the North required a strategy for
bringing the war to an end. The strategy was simple: starve the South
into surrender. Tactically this translated into blockades, sieges, cutting
off supply lines and attacking sources of supply. Anything that supported the strategy of cutting off the South was a valid tactic. If it didn't,
it was a distraction and not to be done.

The American Civil War thinking guided the tactics with absolute clarity.
So, if your vision as a global food manufacturer is about providing 'well-
ness and sustainability', for example, you had better start translating that
into goals and strategic drivers or there will be a whole load of people
thinking, 'Sounds great, but I don't see what it has to do with me!'

Tactics are the actions, projects and initiatives that you and your
team will deliver to create your vision. Developing your tactics needs to
be a systematic activity, not an ad hoc 'to do' list.

1 Look at your key products/services and markets (internal cus-
   tomers) and for each ask these questions:
   → What do we need to do *differently* to be successful?
   → What do we need to *start* doing to be successful?
   → What do we need to *stop* doing to be successful?

2 Look at your SWOT. Which elements do you need to address in
   order to be successful?

3 Make an audit of regular activities and projects. Ask each of your
   people to list their top ten activities and evaluate them in terms of
   the in and out categories above and your products/services and
   markets focus. Ask them to prioritise and develop constructive
   plans for eliminating non-value-adding activities.

4 Create a consolidated list of all actions – grouping and cluster-
   ing them to keep it manageable.

5 Check your goals and KPIs – ensuring that there are actions
   planned to deliver against each of them.

6 Prioritise and agree ownership of each action with your team.

7 Establish a project and portfolio of project management platform.

8 Communicate your strategic action plan to the key stakeholders.

8 DELIVERY *Driving excellence*

Be it in delivery of a new strategy, improving processes or outperform-
ing targets, your reputation as a manager is reliant on your ability to drive
excellence.

Excellence is not a single point or peak of performance, but an ever-
changing aim that needs to be sustained if it is to have a lasting impact
and help you to add real value to the business. The common misconception about excellence is that it is simply delivery against targets. For
sure, targets and KPIs will be the outward measures of your success,
but *they* will change and what excellence is will also have to change to
meet the *new* KPIs.

To do this, you and your team have to not only hit stretching perform-ance targets but also build excellence into your thinking, as though it is in your DNA. In other words, you have to be constantly seeking to be the best.

So how do you build an excellent attitude and behaviour into your cul-ture and everyday mode of operating? Here is an example.

Safety at work!

Working in the production area at a chemical plant, a core driver of every employee is safety. If you are sitting on several thousand tonnes of highly flammable, volatile chemicals, self-preservation will make you very safety-conscious. For the management of the plant, this self-preservation driver is not enough – it is not systematic or rigorous enough and it is too, well, human.

Countless man hours and huge budgets are devoted to inculcating a culture of safety where every employee behaves in a safe manner. The first question that is asked of any action is, 'What are the associ-ated risks?' So, for all vehicles onsite, *nobody* exceeds the site speed limit because speed cameras will catch those who do and they will be banned from driving onsite, no second warning. Even beyond the site, accidents in the home must be reported to the company. All accidents can be avoided and the concept of safety cannot just be switched off and on at the factory gate.

Working in this environment is like entering a different zone, a dif-ferent culture. Outsiders – who do not naturally think about risks and potential problems – initially feel quite uncomfortable. They will look at the safety-conscious team and marvel at the consistent and conscien-tious attention given to *all* aspects of safety.

They get this awareness from the MD, the shop floor and even the canteen workers serving lunch. These guys are *driven* by safety.

Funnily enough, after a (very short) while, the visitor no longer sees this behaviour as extraordinary and even becomes part of the culture – often being more of an advocate and more aware of risk than even the most hardened of the existing team!

So if you are going to drive excellence, you don't just need a few tar-gets, you need to systematically build it into your routines and thinking.

→ Where do I want to be excellent? With the best will in the world, we all have a finite capacity to excel so we need to set ourselves targets.

→ Excellence results from the following. For all your projects and improvements, be aware of the holy trinity of classic project KPIs.

→ **Time**: what is the deadline?
→ **Cost**: how much will it cost to deliver?
→ **Performance**: what benefits will it create?

Results – setting clear objectives

The primary reason for failing to deliver on excellence is the lack of simple clarity on what it actually is. To avoid this pitfall, it is essential that you set clear objectives, which – aligned with your strategy and vision – guide not only the actions but also the measurable qualities of the deliverable that define excellence: time, cost, performance.

The following example is from a marketing manager in a medical devices company who is seeking to drive excellence in the process of securing the listing of the company's products by different regulatory authorities. By the end of next year, the manager aims to have delivered the following:

Objective	Measure	Target
A working system for developing the optimal access strategy per product per country	Populated system in place	All live products have a strategy in place
Improved visibility of the potential value of the pipeline at brand and/or country level	Potential market value (€)	Potential value available for all projects
Improved decision-making on allocation of resources	Rankability of projects against each other	All projects in system
Increase in successful submissions	Prospective monitoring of submissions	Increase over time (no benchmark available)
Increase speed – reduce time to registration	Prospective monitoring of submissions	Decrease over time (no benchmark available)
Achieve target price on submissions	Actual versus planned price	0% deviation
Visibility of status for all applications, by brand and country, available to all internal stakeholders (all priority countries)	Single picture of status of all submissions by brand and country	100% overview

The above table is an example of setting objectives that don't just guide deliverables, but – with clear performance and quality targets – will help target excellence in delivery.

Musts and wants

Too often, staff members are confused by the issue of what is mandatory and what is really important, but, in the final analysis, is just a nice to have. The Fast Track manager will eliminate such confusion and clearly identify:

What we must deliver v. what we want to deliver.

Separate all your objectives into **musts** and **wants**. This is particularly effective when reflecting customer needs.

→ **Must.** Mandatory, measurable, realistic.

→ **Want.** If your objective fails on any of the above, it can only be a want.

→ **Wants.** Can be ranked in importance, depending on whether or not they are required.

So, for example, some musts and wants might be as follows.

→ We will be ISO 9001 compliant – must.

→ We will not exceed budget – must.

→ We will maximise sales – want.

→ We will deliver best-in-class service – want.

The interesting point to recognise here is that wants can seem as important as musts. Any manager would want to maximise areas such as sales or service, and budget and regulatory compliance seem much less sexy, but, if you hit your targets but are not compliant, you and your company will be exposed to sanctions and no amount of increased sales or service will justify that. The best way to look at this is that musts are your ticket to the game, your invitation to play; how you perform against the wants determines whether or not you will win.

When do I set objectives?

Good objectives will clearly guide you towards excellence. So, it is vital that the Fast Track manager sets objectives early enough to influence actions. Objectives are your basic rationale for acting. They are the *why* of your strategy. If you find yourself asking 'Why am I doing this?' after you have started working on something, it is too late. Get the right objectives in place at the very beginning – they will not only enable you to measure progress but also create a basis for effective planning.

Excellent values and behaviours – a question of culture

What matters most in an organisation tends to be results and the common wisdom is that setting clear objectives and KPIs will drive you towards excellence. The Fast Track manager realises that – as with the safety-driven workforce at the chemical plant – excellence will not leap forward from a spreadsheet or a PowerPoint presentation. Instead, it comes from the behaviours, actions and thinking of the team members and the culture they are working in.

As with decision rights, you need to accept the limit to which you as an individual can shape the culture of the team, but do not underestimate your ability to make a change.

 CASE STORY *A CULTURE OF EMPOWERMENT –*
DECISION-MAKING EXCELLENCE, KURT'S STORY

Narrator Kurt was an experienced general manager with a track record of success, which he achieved by getting the best out of his staff. His latest appointment, though, presented him with some challenges.

Context An autocratic leader ran a global electronic components manufacturer in Western Europe for 20 years. Kurt Weber was appointed to the position of vice-president for Europe. As the new vice-president, he was set a series of stretching strategic goals and was keen to deliver.

Issue Kurt needed his team to assume responsibility for a set of initiatives. He was frustrated that, given its history, the team members refused to make decisions without seeking his approval. Worse, projects were starting to fall behind schedule and the global management team was questioning the viability of the EU operation. What made this even harder to understand was the fact that the strategy, roadmap and objectives for delivery had been well documented and agreed with the team.

Solution Kurt recognised that his team had been starved of independence. Faced with the bright light of autonomy, many of them had simply frozen like rabbits in the headlights, while others were simply unable to make decisions.

Kurt decided to install a series of simple processes that would enable his team to perform. He set up decision-making training and templates. He made sure that management reports highlighted key decisions and established ownership. Each week, people held a decision-making session without him. Progress against decisions was integrated into morning meetings. The organisation began to manage itself by its decisions and, eventually, by the quality of its decisions. Finally, it could measure progress by the impact of the decisions on the strategic goals.

Learning Excellence as a word means very little – it needs to be given a tangible aspect. For Kurt, this was in the area of decision-making and its impact on business performance. By making it the centre of every management event, training people and aligning the behaviour with performance and results, excellence in decision-making became part of the fabric of the company.

Excellence within a team – areas for development

As well as decision-making, there is a host of other areas where excellence can be brought to life and embedded into a team's DNA.

The Fast Track manager recognises that core values and basic beliefs are critical to a team's unity and sense of direction. Where values have been agreed at a corporate level, bringing these to life is a great challenge, but the benefits are immense.

→ For every project, identify which values are key.

→ Look at your business's core values and identify with your team which of them are critical to the success of any project or process and how.

→ Write a charter of values for your team after getting members' input as to what matters to them.

Here are some examples of core values:

→ honesty

→ creativity

→ being recognised

→ mutual respect

→ effective and timely communication.

As can be seen, this list is not long and the points are very simple. Keeping it simple is very important. A long list can be misinterpreted. The key thing to remember is not that every potential angle is explored, but the thrust is 'right' and people can easily buy in to it.

Developing a values list with your people is important and so is **communicating** the results to both your boss and other stakeholders, as well as new recruits or people drafted into the team on a part-time basis.

The key to successful communication is to express ideas at the right level for the audience and make sure that messages are clear and understood.

So, when it comes to communication, keep it simple and remember the following.

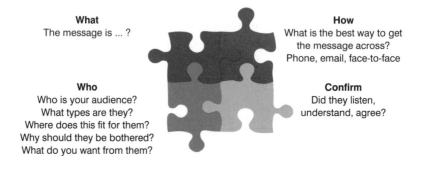

What
The message is ... ?

How
What is the best way to get
the message across?
Phone, email, face-to-face

Who
Who is your audience?
What types are they?
Where does this fit for them?
Why should they be bothered?
What do you want from them?

Confirm
Did they listen,
understand, agree?

Consequences

Creating a consequence-driven environment is perhaps the most effective means of delivering excellence, regardless of changing objectives or any other influence. All rational people are fundamentally driven by the consequences of their actions. As a Fast Track manager, you need to work out what makes people tick and what turns them off. You can then engineer the working environment to provide the positive consequences that will ensure consistent high levels of delivery from key staff.

Here is an example of how this can work.

A section leader reports to her manager the great news that, having worked all weekend and late into the night for the last two weeks, she has completed all the elements of the project that are key to moving forwards. The project is now 20 per cent ahead of schedule and, more importantly, 30 per cent ahead of the performance target without having compromised budget.

The manager is really impressed and tells the section leader what a great job she has done. A week later, he calls the section leader in and transfers the responsibility for a whole workstream of the project to her.

Two months later, the section leader has quit and the project is down the tubes. It is late, the quality of the end product is in jeopardy and the workstream transferred to her ownership has simply gone nowhere.

Like all good managers, the manager carried out an exit interview with the departing section leader. He said that he was sorry to see her go and was interested in understanding why. He was quite shocked to find out that the stress of the last few months had been too much for her to bear. She had been working really hard and done a good job, but the result had been an increase in her workload, which was intolerable and fundamentally unfair – especially as her colleagues on the same pay scale had not been given extra responsibility.

The manager realised that he had rewarded hard work with negative consequences and the impact had been disastrous.

This example is very typical of what happens in the real world: you do a good job and you get rewarded with an increased workload; you do a bad job and (as nobody trusts you) you are rewarded with a decreased workload.

To sustain excellence, the Fast Track manager will reward positive performance with positive consequences. In the example above, it was critical that the project succeeded. Given the expertise and commitment of the section leader, the optimum route would have been to review with her the options for driving the project forwards and reward her performance. These might have included:

→ giving her extra responsibility or workstreams, but reallocating other areas of her job to someone else

→ incorporating the project into her annual review/incentive scheme

→ identifying which areas of the project she felt she could best support and what would need to change to enable this

→ offering time off in lieu for the extra work she had done on the project.

9 DELIVERY *Visibility and control*

One of your challenges as a Fast Track manager will be to focus the performance of your team and, probably, others whom you influence, rather than control, on the things that matter. Earlier in the top ten list, you made strategic decisions and clarified your objectives; you also homed in on what is driving your part of the business and what the overall business wants from you. Visibility and control help to make all this operational. In essence, you will be using the KPIs, first, to drive results, performance and behaviour and, second, to gain confidence that things are actually moving forwards.

First, you should identify the key elements of performance that will deliver your vision and strategy. For the overall organisation, these will typically fall into four areas:

→ **financial** profitability measured by operating income or return on capital

→ **business processes** internal measures of quality and time performance set by the critical business processes

→ **customers** assessment of customers' needs (which may change) and measures of their satisfaction

→ **strategic projects** measures of the progress of new initiatives and business capability improvement in people, systems and procedures.

With reference to your strategic goals and the key issues you are currently trying to resolve in your part of the business, put together a list of the top ten elements that, if measured, would drive your business in the right direction. There should be at least one in each category.

Next, establish measures and targets for those key elements. For many of these indicators, it's often more useful to measure performance earlier in the process to ensure results rather than at the end. For example, if you have a sales target in a business that makes sales on the basis of relationships, you will know that contact with customers is paramount. So, it will be useful to measure the amount of time each salesperson spends with clients.

Set a target towards which you can realistically aim. If the current level of performance is unknown, either carry out benchmarking with other functions (or industry best practice) or agree to review targets after a set period of measuring actual performance. Involve your team in setting the targets. They will often be aspirational and aggressive without any encouragement needed from you.

'If you don't measure it, you don't manage it' is an oft-used phrase in management circles. The Fast Track manager will add, 'If you don't report on it, why did you bother measuring it?' Reports are the basis for successful management. They provide the essential data that feed effective decision-making and enable the Fast Track manager to track progress and improvements in the delivery of strategy.

Having said this, reports do have something of a bad press. They are seen as hard or too wordy to read and often have no relevance. Writing them is even harder. Resist the temptation to indulge in long expositions of how a situation is developing if your report is to have impact.

When setting expectations for a report, be clear about the following aspects.

→ **Objectives.** Why is this report important? What will it be used for? For example, a project portfolio report will enable decisions to be made about investment and prioritisation.

→ **Key information.** What information must be provided to enable you to understand the issues within the report? An example might be housekeeping data, such as owner, department, cost centre.

→ **KPIs.** What is the report actually measuring? What variables are going to drive decision-making according to status?

→ **Action.** Reports will not just reflect the situation but also offer solutions and an opportunity for the report writer to add value beyond the raw data included.

Consider the example below of a project portfolio report from a soft drinks manufacturer and note the following.

→ It shows clearly the areas of concern and quickly highlights actions and options – use of colour (red–amber–green) is very powerful as it helps the reader to focus in on those areas of the report that are dynamic and specifically those that are of concern.

→ It does not merely highlight the problem but also suggests solutions.

→ It fits on one page. The Fast Track manager knows the value of the one-page solution, even if it is often easier to say more!

→ It is not trying to measure too much. As such, it does not exceed the bandwidth of either the team or the reader.

Brand	Category	Brand manager	Quality	Timing	Budget	Issues	Planned actions	Options
Tarm	Soft drink	DW	60%	AHEAD	ON	Flavour	None	R&D new flavour
Catem Spring	Water	JK	80%	BEHIND	OVER	Bottle design not agreed	Revert to old format	Invest in new plant?
RingT	Juice	RB	45%	ON	UNDER	Lack of premium taste	New supplier	Accept taste and drive other qualities

Review and challenge

The final part of maintaining progress is accountability. Having identified the critical areas of your business to measure and established a reporting process, you must make sure that individuals in your team understand that you really mean it. This means regular reviews of the reports, recognition for those who have performed well and challenges being made to those who appear to be struggling. Where people are not delivering, it is often because they are working on other stuff and have not yet got the message that your 'stuff' is more important. Your job is to keep the team focused on the numbers that matter to **you**.

Financials

Whatever else happens in a business, the financial aspects will generally be the best-understood ones (though not always well!) Ultimately, financial performance is *the* measure of the success of any business, so it's important to know what you need to control and be well versed in the financial jargon for your business. Spend time with the accountants in the business and find out what's driving them. Also, get to know what numbers the senior managers in the business are focused on. Just like you, they will have made some decisions about what numbers will help them strategically and, like you, they'll be happy to know that you are contributing to them.

10 DELIVERY *Taking control*

'Where is the wisdom we have lost in knowledge? Where is the knowledge we have lost in information?' This quote from the poet T.S. Eliot (from *The Rock*, part 1, 1934), writing more than 70 years ago, shows that making decisions in a sea of data is not a new thing. Though we certainly have significantly more data to deal with today, taking control is about extracting what matters to a given situation so that we can apply our wisdom to effective problem solving and decision-making. It is also about managing the performances of your team members, knowing how to deal with those who aren't delivering to your expectations.

Effective meetings

Meetings often get a bad press.

I wasn't sure what we were trying to achieve or why I was there – and I wasn't the only one!

The meeting went on for too long – we could have got through it in half the time.

As usual, on at least half the actions, nobody had done anything since the last meeting.

Making meetings effective, though, is relatively simple. The purpose of any meeting will be to share issues, track progress, make decisions and gain buy-in. They are of differing types and vary in size, but here are some simple rules for running effective meetings.

Before the meeting

→ Consider whether a meeting is actually required. Could you do this in a smaller meeting? Do you need to involve this many people? Could you make a decision legitimately on your own?

→ Issue an agenda (use POST – see the Director's toolkit, page 201).

During the meeting

→ Appoint a note-taker. Running meetings *and* taking minutes is a difficult juggling act.

→ Review any actions set at a previous meeting.

→ Capture minutes live – using a laptop, LCD, whiteboard is easy and immediately visible.

→ Allocate tasks – who, what, when.

→ Measure meeting performance v. planned outcomes.

After the meeting

→ Issue the minutes – as soon as possible.

→ Periodically chase progress on the action points.

QUICK TIP *CHAIRING GOOD MEETINGS*

If you struggle to keep meeting discussions under control and your meetings tend to overrun, seek permission from the group to chair the meeting aggressively. They'll prefer a shorter meeting and you can politely interrupt long discussions.

Critical thinking

This is one of the key differences between effective and less effective managers. Most of us think intuitively – that is, we don't consciously follow a process – but a quick deconstruction of good managers in action reveals that, to a greater or lesser degree, they are using a process to analyse information and make decisions.

Let us take a look at four critical thinking tools.

Prioritise

You will, no doubt, have had experience of crises that needed to be managed, 'fires' that needed to be put out or just an overly full to-do list. You will also have observed some managers are better than others at managing these situations and that is most likely because they add structure to a difficult and possibly slightly panicky situation.

Here is how it works:

1 List all the issues in the context of the environment in which you're working. This could be all the stuff you have in your mind at the start of a very busy day or a data dump at the start of a brainstorm or crisis meeting or else items for discussion in a review meeting.

2 Rate each item in terms of its importance (seriousness) and urgency (deadlines). These ratings are relative to others on the list and could be kept simply to H for high, M for medium and L for low. This will enable you to prioritise the issues on the list so that you can tackle the most important and urgent (H/H) items first. In a crisis, many things may *seem* urgent, but this analysis will point up those that are not also *important* (see also the importance and urgency matrix once more on page 56).

3 Agree what action should be taken and who is responsible. In a well-run prioritising meeting, it might be appropriate that people now leave to investigate and work through the next stages in the process – that is, analyse and decide on what has been allocated to them, reporting back on progress at the next meeting.

Use this approach when there are a lot of issues to work through and especially if there is pressure to move quickly – thinking before doing is never a bad approach. You can also use this process for collecting and sorting through issues and ideas at the start of a strategic review or project planning meeting.

Analyse

One of the more important things you can do as a manager is to challenge assumptions and what we might call 'received truths' – things that people take for granted in your organisation. Decisions and actions are often based on these assumptions and, if they are wrong or just politically expedient, they can do significant damage.

Let us look at an example to clarify this point.

Bob House, the regional manager of a chain of women's clothes shops in the south of England, was concerned that one of the branches was showing a sharp decline in business. He'd had to discuss this at a board meeting and, thinking about recent changes that might be relevant, he quickly pointed out that a new district manager, Helen, had been appointed to run this branch along with six others. She'd arrived just before the decline in sales and Bob and the Board quickly came to the conclusion that she must be to blame. Bob left with little doubt about what he was expected to do.

Next day, he was out with one of his team, Matt, visiting shops and talking through the issues. They had enjoyed a long and trusting relationship and Bob valued the opportunity to share the burden of a tricky task with an old friend. Matt was uncomfortable – not with the nature of the conversation, but with the data surrounding the decision. 'Surely, if it was Helen's fault, all *seven* branches in her district would be affected. It doesn't make sense. What's different about the Wisborough branch relative to the others in that district?' A little further into the conversation, they recalled that the major employer in Wisborough had closed its factory, resulting in massive local unemployment.

When, later still, Bob talked to Helen she confirmed that all the shops in Wisborough had been suffering from the fall in disposable income in the area and she outlined her plan for the survival of their shop ...

So, if you have this problem with your team, challenge the assumptions and ask for more rigour in the analysis. When, with a little more thought, you and they know that an assumed cause of a problem doesn't really stack up, encourage them to challenge it and dig further.

As Helen might have told you under different circumstances, decisions based on false causes can be very damaging to a business.

Decide

Decisions can be complicated by a number of factors:

→ too many choices

→ too many opinions

→ unclear criteria

→ high risks associated with the output

→ conflict over the options.

Sometimes the decision is actually avoided. Of course, this is not really avoiding the decision, it's unconsciously making the decision that the status quo is the best option. So, it pays to use some kind of structure in your decision-making.

Think about the type of decision you're making.

→ **Binary.** Yes or no; go or no go, such as should we continue with the launch or should we buy a new house?

→ **Alternatives.** A range of mutually exclusive alternatives from which one must be chosen, such as which house should we buy or to which location should we move the office?

→ **Features.** A range of options from which you need to pick a number of top-performing ones, such as which extras should we get with our new car or how can we reduce the amount of time spent in the product development process?

Then structure your thinking (explicitly if you are working with a group; implicitly if on your own) to separate out the criteria that will help you make a choice and the options from which to choose (see a more detailed process in the Director's toolkit, page 201).

Protect

Having taken considerable trouble to make your decision, including identifying it as a priority and being clear about the cause you may be trying to resolve, it would be a shame not to protect it by thinking about any risks that might be associated with it. This step applies equally to any initiatives you are leading or proposals you are making. Any senior manager is going to be reassured if you can demonstrate that you have considered the risks (for more information, see the Director's toolkit, page 201).

Managing poor performance

Poor work performance by individuals makes it difficult for you and your team to achieve your goals. In addition, failure to address poor performance will cause resentment and have a negative impact on those employees who are performing satisfactorily. Managing poor work performance should therefore be part of an overall performance management process that also includes carrying out regular appraisals and identifying and meeting learning and development needs (as discussed above). Dealing with poor perfromance requires a focus on understanding the cause of the problem along with a plan to overcome it.

Let's think first about the causes of poor performance or falling performance standards. You must identify the reasons for this so that you can tailor your support to help the employee address specific problems.

There are a number of factors that can dictate whether or not an individual *performer* delivers an *action* to an expected performance level. If you can gain clarity regarding all of these factors, then the individual concerned is very likely to deliver what is required. Here are some key questions to ask if you're trying to uncover the causes of poor performance.

→ How clear are the performance expectations and were they understood and agreed? In other words, does the individual know precisely what is expected and has he or she agreed that it can be done? If they are not clear, the individual concerned may actually believe that he or she has done a good job and may have a right to be confused by your admonitions.

→ Is he or she affected by environmental noise? This might include a difficult (perhaps too noisy) working environment, the wrong equipment to do the job or conflicting demands on his or her time.

→ Does the individual have the required skills and knowledge and is well suited to the task?

→ Does he or she get a balance of positive to negative consequences on completing the task (briefly described earlier under 8 Delivery Driving excellence, page 78)? If the balance of consequences is more towards the negative than the positive, he or she may choose not to do the task again or do it differently.

→ Does he or she receive useful feedback to help improve performance? For example, do you, as the person's manager, give clear and detailed feedback on the job that has just been done, indicating areas for improvement and rewards for good performance?

If you analyse poor performance in this way, you will get an objective understanding of the reasons behind it, from which you can work out how to take action. Let's look at an example.

Jo works in a call centre offering customer service and dealing with complaints. It's a busy, noisy place with a very spirited sales team at one end of the room and as many as 150 people on the floor in total.

Her department has taken on a new piece of software to help employees deal more effectively with customers and improve the logging and analysis of issues and complaints. Jo's boss, Adrian, thinks the new software is wonderful and is very frustrated with Jo because, as far as he can see, she is not enthusiastic about the new process and avoids using it wherever possible. Adrian has got to the point of talking to the human resources department about taking disciplinary action against Jo, but could he take a different tack?

Let's have a look.

→ **How clear are the performance expectations and were they understood and agreed?** Well, Jo has been told to use the new system for all her calls, so that seems to be OK.

→ **Are the employees affected by environmental noise?** It is a difficult place to work if you're trying to have a sympathetic chat with a customer, but others manage it and they don't have other things to do that might compete with their time. So, another tick.

→ **Do they have the required skills and knowledge and are they well suited to the task?** Hmmm. Jo received a five-minute intro to the new system and how to use it with the rest of the team. They were told it is intuitive and that they'd pick it up in no time, but Jo has struggled with this. She has asked for help, but Adrian is 'too busy'. The team doesn't have any technical support and the others are all too busy to help each other. Jo is not confident about using the system while talking to her customer.

→ **Do they get a balance of positive consequences on completing the task?** Not really. Jo feels silly asking the customers some of the questions on the system and the customers immediately get frustrated with her. Because she likes to get on with the call, she often gets behind in completing the boxes in the system, which means that she takes fewer calls than the others. No bonus for her!

→ **Do they receive useful feedback to help them improve their performance?** Well, she does get feedback from customers, but it is not particularly useful in terms of helping her work out what to do, so that doesn't count. When was the last time Adrian sat down with her and congratulated her for dealing well with a difficult customer (something she is very good at)? Too long ago and he hasn't done anything to build on this and develop her confidence to combine this skill with the new skills needed to work the system.

If you were in Adrian's position, what would you do? Hopefully, you have moved from, 'Jo's being awkward and refuses to move with the times and use the new system' to, 'Jo hasn't had any training or support on the job, it interrupts the good work she does with customers and she has received no feedback or coaching support from me.'

The former statement is subjective and prejudicial, giving you few options *but* it would be ill-advised to pursue disciplinary procedures, while the latter identifies specific causes against which you, the manager, can plan specific actions and help Jo to improve performance.

It is not always this easy or clear, but people don't usually come to work to do a bad job, so, as a manager, your role is to find out how a person is falling short in performance, what causes lie behind that failing and what you can do to change the situation.

Fast Track top ten summary

If you are going to make a difference in management, you need to do this in a structured and targeted way. Most importantly, you will need to determine where and how you can add maximum value and then **deliver**. Use the Fast Track top ten to set your strategy, secure the resources and support you need and drive the systematic delivery of excellence.

STOP – THINK – ACT

This chapter has covered a variety of tools and techniques used by Fast Track managers to optimise their performance and that of their teams. Some may have been more relevant to you than others and some may need to be adapted to suit your specific situation. Most managers will make some use of all of these tools at some point in their careers, though not necessarily all at once. Take some time now to reflect on the top ten management tools and techniques and identify elements that you will work on to improve your management performance.

What should we do?	What tools and techniques are appropriate?
Who do we need to involve?	Who else needs to be involved to make it work and why?
What resources will we require?	What information, facilities, materials, equipment or budget will be required and are they available?
What is the timing?	When will this change be implemented? Is there a deadline?

Visit **www.Fast-Track-Me.com** to use the Fast Track online planning tool.

Managing by means of budgets

Professor Carol Print Henley Business School, University of Reading

Organisations could be considered as a stream of managerial decisions. These involve many aspects of the business – marketing, purchasing, production, finance and so on. It is therefore critical to both recognise the interrelatedness of many decisions and coordinate the decision-making, as the management of these issues will have an impact on the bottom line and performance. This process of coordination is usually managed via the budgeting process and organisations that do not effectively plan, control and monitor their decision-making are unlikely to achieve their operational targets and strategic business objectives.

Budgeting has been considered a management tool for many years. It evolved in the 1920s to help organisations plan capital requirements and manage their scarce resources and assist managers in fulfilling their stewardship role. In later years, budgeting developed into a process to enable financial managers to control and evaluate managerial performance. There has been questioning of the budgeting process for some years in recognition of the need to manage where competitive conditions are not stable, product lifecycles are shortening, customer loyalty may be more fickle and competition tougher. Jack Welch, former CEO of General Electric, wrote the following in *Fortune* magazine in 1995:

The budget is the bane of corporate America. It should never have existed. A budget is this: if you make it, you generally get a pat on the back and a few bucks. If you miss it, you get a stick in the eye – or worse ... Making a budget is an exercise in minimalisation. You're always trying to get the lowest out of people, because everyone is negotiating to get the lowest number.

While there is little argument that the original intention of budgeting – providing a forecast of expenditures and revenues for a specific period of time that could be compared with the actual results – is sound, there are changes affecting the soundness of this process. The structure of organisations has become more complicated and organisations are operating in highly competitive and rapidly changing business environments. This could result in organisations using budgets that are inaccurate and incomplete, while incurring considerable cost in their preparation. There has been a change from a budget being a tool of financial planning and control to the function, scope and management of a budget becoming much more complex.

A number of studies provide views of this management process. One, conducted by Price Waterhouse in large multinational organisations in the 1990s, identified the significant cost and time involved. On average, it was found that budget preparation took 110 days from start to finish and profit forecasts varied from actual results by an average of 10 per cent. Another found that the budgeting process takes up around 20 to 30 per cent of managers' and controllers' time. Yet another identified that a majority of finance directors were dissatisfied with the budgeting process. Nonetheless, others indicate that 99 per cent of all companies in Europe still operate with formal budgeting systems.

Many companies are looking for ways to improve their planning processes by 'better budgeting' – that is, making better use of different approaches to budgeting. Some principal areas of disquiet relate to the time-consuming and costly nature of budgeting, the lack of strategic focus (because of the emphasis on cost and not value creation), 'game playing' and the perceived need to meet the budget, which may mean not responding, changing and being as flexible as the organisation should.

Others have taken a more revolutionary approach – often referred to as 'beyond budgeting' – and there are a number of well-known Scandinavian multinational companies, such as Svenska Handelsbanken, Borealis, Statoil and IKEA, that have abandoned traditional budgeting in favour of the use of scorecards, activity-based management, rolling forecasts and trend reporting. This involves the abandonment of an annual planning cycle and removing the parts of budgeting that are considered bureaucratic and time-costly in favour of forecasts that encourage flexibility, improvement and responsiveness.

EXPERT VOICE

TECHNOLOGIES

To remain as effective and efficient as possible, Fast Track managers differentiate themselves by the support mechanisms they put in place to help themselves and their team. This includes the intelligent use of appropriate technology, enabling, for example, the automation of non-core activities, thereby freeing up time to focus on managing, motivating and leading their teams. It may also include the use of coaches, peer-to-peer networks and gaining access to the latest thinking in their field.

Getting started

Why consider technology?

There are a number of reasons for this.

→ The rate of change in the external environment is dramatic. In all industries, we see the consolidation of competition, pressures from international markets, emerging new technology and relentless changes in legislation. How can we possibly keep up and remain aware of what is going on?

→ There is certainly no shortage of information – frankly, there is too much. How do we sift through the myriad of junk emails, websites, free journals and texts that arrive uninvited at all times of the day and night?

→ While information overload is a critical issue, the reality also is that if we don't make use of relevant and up-to-date information, we will fall behind the competition. Technology may not be the answer to all our problems, but it is a very important enabler, helping us remain effective and efficient.

What activities should we focus on?

Before deciding how to use technology or automation to save time, eliminate – or at least identify – low-value or unnecessary activities. This is vital to prevent you from automating illogical or time-wasting activities and building them permanently into your business process.

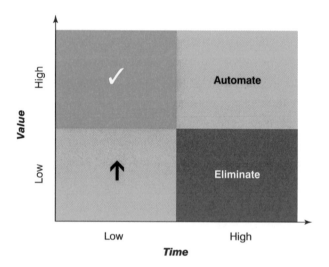

Start by making a list of all the current activities undertaken by your business teams. Then assess how much time and resources are spent on each item, plus the value you associate with each – perhaps using a simple five-point scale. Then draw a simple two-by-two matrix (such as the above) to assess where each activity falls.

→ Those falling in the bottom right-hand corner are the ones that it is critical to address – those using up a lot of time and resources but producing little of value. Eliminate these. Perhaps, for example, there are idea review meetings you don't need to attend or some that could be delegated to a member of your team, which might also be good for his or her personal development.

→ Those in the bottom left-hand corner pose a problem. They are not consuming much time, so are reasonably efficient, but they are not delivering a lot of value either. Perhaps there is a way of improving the value of each activity. You might, for example, change the agenda for a regular management meeting to include asking the team to come up with at least one new idea for an improvement that could be made.

→ Activities in the top left-hand box are already efficient and of high value. Perhaps they are already automated, so leave them until your next review.

→ In the top right-hand box are the high-value, time-consuming activities. They make a big difference, but take a lot of time to do, such as analysis of the market data or internal performance indicators. These are, by definition, important, high-value items, so you do not want to get rid of them, but you need to find efficient ways of doing them. 'Automation' may be achieved using technology, such as using a Web subscription service to send monthly updates on competitors direct to your desktop rather than you having to search the internet for new data. Alternatively, it might be as simple as changing the way a regular activity is done to reduce the time and effort required, such as using video conferencing to conduct monthly idea-generation meetings with distributors.

Think carefully about your overall management of time. Be aware of how you use it and constantly look for ways of improving this. Once you have formally conducted the time-value assessment above, you will be more conscious of this need.

Don't forget that we tend to do those things we enjoy and put off what is less fun. So, if you're serious about putting technology to the best possible use, then try to overcome this psychological bias and look at how you use your time as objectively as you can. If you do not manage your time well, you will find it difficult to fit in any innovation tasks, for example, because they don't impact your short-term objectives.

When invited to meetings, constantly ask the question, 'Why?' What value will the meeting be to you or what value will you bring to it? If there is no obvious answer, then review the objectives or role with the organiser or other stakeholders. If you still don't get the 'Why?' decline the invitation or delegate. The key is to remove unnecessary tasks and activities before looking for opportunities to automate. That way, you avoid putting IT and other resources into something that has little or no value.

Finally, encourage your team to carry out the same exercise so that, when you are deciding on various options for automation, you increase the overall effectiveness of the *team*, not just yourself.

The process–system link

How should we use information technology (IT)?

Think carefully about how you will use technology and ensure that it links back to what you are seeking to achieve. Perhaps the starting point is to look at your overall business framework for opportunities to make each element quicker, simpler and, possibly, more fun!

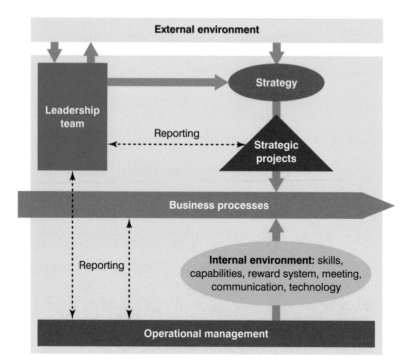

Some aspects of the framework will lend themselves to the use of technology, whereas some of the softer areas, such as leadership and culture, will offer fewer opportunities to do so.

Make sure that the information provided is accurate and timely so that you have confidence in acting on it. Think carefully also about security – who will be using the technology, what information will it contain and how sensitive is the data? Most aspects of IT are becoming more secure, but you need to take time to ensure that you set them up correctly in the first place and have the appropriate level of security.

Top technology

How do I know what technology exists?

So, now that you understand the need for technology, systems and automation and where you are going to deploy them for best effect, how do you find out what is available?

Get into the habit of scanning for technology trends on the Web, in industry journals or at trade fairs and exhibitions. Look at what other people in your business are reading – particularly those you most admire. Where do they get their information? Take time to understand what other firms, perhaps even your competitors or suppliers, are using.

Be aware, however, that there is a lot of information available and new technology is coming along all the time. How do you decide what is relevant and what is useful? Start with a healthy scepticism. Investigate the technology, but ask the 'So what?' question. Is this relevant to my team and me? How will it impact performance?

The impact of technology on business today is very different from that of only ten years ago. It is also more challenging for most of us to get a grip on what is happening technologically and, more importantly, form a vision of what might happen. Depending on the size of your business and the scale of the opportunity presented by technology, it may be worth employing someone to advise you on the way forward. This could be a permanent employee with vision and technical knowledge or it might be a consultant who has a good overview of the world you work in and may have a clearer idea of what might be required.

What tools will support management in the longer term?

Recognise that developments in technology are happening so quickly that the list of what is available to you will never be static. Use the list below to challenge what is possible, but accept that it is a snapshot of what is happening at a point in time.

QUICK TIP *PROCESS V. VISION*

Creativity and routine can seem mutually exclusive, but you need *both*. Find people in your team to champion each element of strategic delivery and set goals that will integrate new ideas into business-as-usual.

1 Strategic project tracker

What is it?	Project and portfolio management (PPM) software applications are used to scope, plan, monitor and control the implementation of projects arising from strategic decisions. They provide a structured approach to managing a portfolio of complex projects. Strategic initiatives should be viewed as projects and need to be planned as such – too many fail to deliver, or just peter out, often because they are poorly project managed.
Pros	PPM software provides a very effective way of planning the overall portfolio of project activities, making it clear what the individual priorities are. It sets out specific objectives and, ultimately, who does what and when. Simple outputs can also provide a clear communication mechanism for all stakeholders. Web-based applications used across an organisation also provide a means of managing a portfolio of projects as a whole, as opposed to managing individual projects in isolation.
Cons	Some project management tools are too complex for strategic projects. They tend to focus on detailed task and resource management as opposed to the typical success factors, such as having clear objectives, an effective stakeholder management process and a simple risk register.
Success factors	Find a simple and easy-to-use Web-based software product and ensure that key people know how to use it. Finally, don't forget that project and portfolio management is as much about setting the vision and leading the team as plotting the critical path.
Example	The Web-based report below shows all of the strategic projects within a region. A simple red–amber–green classification is used to identify projects needing attention. During a review meeting, the team will 'drill down' into the detail of projects needing support.

Ref.	Title	Description	Owner	Lead Team	% complete	Period	Budget	Project NPV	Start	Close	STATUS	Issues	Stage		
Change Management															
1	ABC Supply chain DEMO	Streamlining electronic ordering using integrated web-based order management system	Bruce (Andy)	Operations	64	2009-Q2	£10,000	£450,167	13 Mar 2009	7 Aug 2009	1-Red	2	2. Measure		
2	Innovation process	Introduction of cross-business ideas and innovation process	Badeley (George)	Logistics and Supply Chain	54	2009-Q4	£20,000	£386,167	6 Jan 2009	17 Aug 2009	2-Amber	2	1. Define		
3	Project management infrastructure	The development of org, structure, processes, performance systems and report systems needed to support the delivery of DAL's strategic project portfolio	Project Office(KT)	Service and Support	20	2009-Q3	£70,000	£339,510	16 Mar 2009	16 Sep 2009	2-Amber		3. Analyse		
							£100,000	£1,175,844	6 Jan 2009	16 Sep 2009	1-Red				
Continuous Improvement															
4	Internal communications	Improvement of internal comms through use of the new intranet	Bruce (Andy)	Logistics and Supply Chain	56	2009-Q4	£5,000	£145,608	30 Jan 2009	7 Aug 2009	2-Amber	2	3. Analyse		
							£5,000	£145,608	30 Jan 2009	7 Aug 2009	2-Amber				
Information Technology															
5	Cross-functional learning	Database system to capture and transfer operational insights across functions	Welsford (Barry)	Logistics and Supply Chain	60	2009-Q3	£10,000	£350,167	6 Jan 2009	7 Aug 2009	3-Green	2	5. Control		
							£10,000	£350,167	6 Jan 2009	7 Aug 2009	3-Green				

2 Websites – trade sites, business news, business communities

What is it?

The internet provides a wide range of valuable resources for the Fast Track manager. The challenge is to know *what* to look for and *where* to get the most *value*. Useful websites will include trade sites specialising in some aspect of your business sector, business news sites, giving the latest information, and general information from sites such as Wikipedia.

Pros

The internet is a rich source of information on a variety of topics, information that is often free and quick to get hold of. It can provide a wealth of information about customers and competitors in a matter of minutes where previously it would have taken weeks. It encourages creativity, as remarked by Franklin P. Adams: 'I find that a great part of the information I have was acquired by looking up something and finding something else on the way.' There is also the added benefit of social networking with other like-minded people or communities of practice.

Cons

Most of the information contains a degree of bias and may not have been validated by a publisher. After all, they may have produced it for their own purposes. It is also typically unstructured, in that a search on a topic will yield lots of results, but the information on each site will be laid out in a different style. Some people call it a repository of several trillion words; the trouble lies in locating the 25 words you really need. Wikipedia, for example, is a good source, but if you are going to depend on a piece of data in it you probably need to check it with another source.

Success factors

Use the Web as a rich source of information and get into the habit of reviewing competitors' and customers' sites regularly. Beware of information overload and, if new information is of critical importance, then validate your conclusions using other sources. A neat rule of thumb is the one that journalists use: only publish a 'fact' if you have got at least two reliable sources. Also, don't forget to delegate. Try asking one of your team to locate five 'useful' pieces of information per week from the Web.

3 Internet networking tools

What is it?

There are various websites the purpose of which is connecting with people or having online discussions (blogs). Networking sites such as Facebook and LinkedIn are powerful for keeping in touch with colleagues and customers and answering questions or recruiting. They often have industry-specific groups to facilitate networking in that sector. Blogs (industry chatrooms) are special websites that allow people to log in and discuss ideas relating to a specific topic in the form of a discussion thread where the most recent comments are displayed first.

Pros

Social sites are a great way to keep in touch with colleagues, resources and customers, especially if they move companies. They can be a very useful way to find out what's going on in your business area or to use for more specific things, such as recruitment. You can use them to 'advertise', but you need to be careful not to break any house rules relating to being too overtly commercial. Blogs provide a more open form of discussion than emails as the discussion can be seen by others and is captured for future reference by other teams.

Cons

These sites are public, so obviously they aren't suitable for private or confidential information or discussions. If you find yourself invited by someone you don't really want to connect to, you don't have to accept an invitation. Unless there is a clear reason for going to a blog, many people just don't bother. This means that blogs can be populated by people who just want to be 'on the Web'. That said, it doesn't mean they are of no value; it just means you have to evaluate opinions and perspectives carefully.

Success factors

Consider carefully whether or not to use a social network and, if so, how? How would you focus it on specific business needs or problems? What would make it exciting and worthwhile enough for it to work when most people will have other commitments to focus on? Perhaps find a small team that would be interested in piloting a blog on a specific topic and see how they get on.

4 Communication tools

What is it?

Email has become the standard form of communication across and within businesses. It is now a key, if not essential, tool for effective communications. Other communication tools include presentation and document packages such as PowerPoint and Word.

Pros

The nature of email allows for a less formal writing style and brief interchanges. Communication by this means is immeasurably faster than post, which means that an email conversation can resolve issues in minutes. Critically, emails get on to the recipients' desktops and stay there until they have been read (or actioned), unlike a traditional letter, which goes through many filters. Used well, presentation and document software can produce powerful communications in a variety of media – print, electronic and projected. Good use of these tools can help you make your case more effectively than would otherwise be possible.

Cons   Email can have negative impact in three ways: people may copy in a range of others for information or political reasons, which means that you will receive emails you don't need; email has, for some, replaced face-to-face or phone contact, which are still essential forms of communication; the immediacy of emails means that people are distracted by short-term issues at the expense of longer-term priorities, which require focus and concentration for longer periods.

Success factors   Use email selectively to direct members of the team and communicate with key stakeholders. Don't use email exclusively, in place of face-to-face or phone communication – these are more motivating for your team than email. Help your team/business manage its email culture. Emails should, ideally, be dealt with at certain points in the day so that people are not distracted from other activities. When preparing presentations and reports, keep them brief and remember to have the recipient in mind when you write them.

QUICK TIP *TAKE RISKS*

If you avoid every risk associated with your strategy, you will not achieve very much. Map potential risks according to the value they may deliver, then go for the ones that are the least risky and deliver the highest rewards. Be sure to identify and prevent potential causes of risk, developing mitigating actions in case the risk becomes a reality.

5 Spreadsheets

What is it?   Spreadsheets are useful ways to prepare and present data and work with the numerical aspects of a business, particularly the financial ones. Budgeting and forecasting will often be done in this way.

Pros   The simplicity and widespread nature of these tools means that their value as powerful business tools can be overlooked. There is no easier way to make financial plans, do quick forecasts or prepare graphical presentations of your data. Also, almost everyone has access to the software to read them.

Cons

As the complexity of a spreadsheet application increases and it becomes more embedded in your business's processes, it can take significant amounts of effort to keep it up to date. People may not recognise the power of automating the process at this point and will become bogged down in completing spreadsheets and manipulating data.

Success factors

Keep your (and your team's) spreadsheets simple so that they have the maximum impact. Consider automating the spreadsheet by upgrading to a Web-based tool if this application becomes central to your business processes.

6 People tools – personality profiling and development tools

What is it?

People development tools have been around for some time, but these have recently become much more accessible through Web-based and electronic applications and are therefore of more immediate use. Tools include personality profiles (such as Insights Discovery), which highlight your personality traits, including strengths and weaknesses; forums for 360° feedback (this is feedback from your boss, your peers and your reports) and web-tools for personal performance development management.

Pros

Developing your team (or yourself) can be much more effective if self-awareness is increased. The ease of access to these tools makes initiatives such as 360° feedback very easy to administer and personal performance trackers can increase the transparency of individual development activities.

Cons

There is generally a cost associated with these tools, though it may not be great. The ease of access doesn't mean that the content is any easier to deal with – after all, this is all about people. Personality profiles and particularly 360° feedback can give you frank information about yourself that could be illuminating to the point of distress.

Success factors

Use these tools in the context of a carefully planned and structured initiative and make sure that professional support is available to help debrief people about their profiles and feedback reports.

7 Video and web conferencing

What is it?

Video and web conferencing allow people to communicate with voice and video as well as sharing images on their computers, even if the other person is located elsewhere in the world (or just working from home) – rather like having a telephone conversation with someone and being able to see them at the same time. This technology has been around for a long time, but, with increased internet speeds and improved flatscreen displays, it is getting cheaper and better all the time. Skype, MSN and powwownow are examples of free-to-use systems that have been adopted by millions worldwide and are run from your own laptop or computer.

Pros	The obvious advantage is that they cut down on travel, reducing financial and environmental costs and freeing up your time. Some systems will also tell you when the other person is available and personal desktop-based systems are convenient and very easy to use. On a practical level, sharing a desktop on the Web enables several people to edit a single document at the same time – a real step forward from comparing a document over the phone.
Cons	Within small groups, small free-to-use systems work well, but setting up large-scale, group video conferencing facilities can be expensive. Many systems just do not offer the quality required for effective communications. They are often very impersonal and so, even when the quality of the signal is good, it does not provide personal contact, so can be ineffective in, for example, creative sessions where resolving conflict and gaining consensus will be important.
Success factors	Investigate internet-based technologies and consider using a standard version in a pilot situation – within a small team, for example – in order to work out whether or not this technology is appropriate and, if so, how you want to use it. You will need to establish management routines in terms of what to use and when in order to make it effective.

8 Enterprise resource planning systems

What is it?	Enterprise resource planning (ERP) systems are intended to manage all the information and functions of a business or company. Such systems typically handle the manufacturing, logistics, distribution, inventory, shipping, invoicing and accounting for a company. ERP software can aid in the control of many business activities, including sales, marketing, delivery, invoicing, production, inventory management, quality management and human resource management.
Pros	An ERP system eliminates redundant data and procedural operations. This increases efficiency in the business. The great power of ERP systems is that they can yield very useful and complete data for management teams, enabling faster and more informed decision-making. With ERP, it should also be possible to observe trends in the data, anticipating problems before they are out of control.
Cons	ERP systems involve huge investments of money and time for a business, so, once installed, changes or major revisions can be very costly. As a result, ERP systems can be seen as inflexible and not supportive of local business processes.
Success factors	Sometimes you will be involved in making the decision to implement an ERP system, but, more likely, you will be working with a system that has been implemented from above. In this situation, your best approach is to work constructively with the implementation, choosing judiciously when to advocate changes and when to accept compromise. Don't forget the powerful political weight that lies behind a centralised ERP implementation.

9 Functional performance and reporting systems

What is it?	Tools that support and enable performance in different functions. There is no single application here, but a variety of tools, depending on the application. In a sales function, examples would be Salesforce.com and customer relationship management (CRM) databases. These tools help staff to do their jobs better and provide management information to help you improve the performance of the team.
Pros	These systems encourage a more structured way of working and will help you to introduce some sort of process into aspects of your business that might otherwise be missing. They can be intuitive for the users and will help them perform better in their jobs. As a manager, you should be able to use the information from these tools to monitor and control performance more objectively. Any such system should be able to provide a dashboard, which shows performance against known KPIs.
Cons	It is all too easy to impose a system on your team that doesn't give them what they need or they see as restrictive. If the benefits aren't clear, people will resist it. There may be a temptation to massage the tool, but the focus must remain on the business results.
Success factors	Make sure that you are clear about whatever business process or activity (in terms of outputs and steps) you are going to automate. If you are not, you will probably end up with a system that doesn't deliver what you need. Involve your team in the design and/or decision-making of the new tool. They are much more likely to be advocates for it if they have been responsible for its implementation.

10 Mobile technology

What is it?	The rapid advances in mobile technology mean that managers can now access on their telephones or PDAs or smart phones pretty much anything that could be accessed on a computer. Most phones designed for business use will now give you access to the internet, your emails and more specific applications.
Pros	You're never out of touch. You can keep abreast of email activity that relates to you, ensuring that you respond in a timely manner. You can use otherwise 'dead time', such as when travelling, to deal with your emails. You can also do urgent internet research while on the move.
Cons	You're never out of touch. There may be an assumption in the business that you can respond immediately to any email. This can upset your agenda for the day, steer you away from high-importance/low-urgency activities and be very disruptive in meetings where people may appear more interested in their mobiles than the content of the meeting.

Success factors	Try to manage your mobile rather than the other way around. There may be an emergency situation that requires you to monitor emails for a short period, but, otherwise, limit your access to the email function (just as you should when you are at your computer), keep emails in the context of your strategic objectives and set rules for your team about the use of mobiles in meetings.

CASE STORY ACT DIFFERENT – TOOLS AND PEOPLE, MIKE'S STORY

Narrator Mike was a sales manager for a global electronic components business. He loved the pressure and creativity of sales, but wasn't sure where his long-term career was heading.

Context The business had just bought a major competitor, so it was an exciting time. New products and new customers meant business was about to become a lot busier and, hopefully, a lot more profitable.

Issue The new portfolio of technology available to Mike and his sales team was actually beginning to become a burden. The senior managers were looking for a quick return on the merger costs – either in the form of job cuts or increased sales. There may have been a whole lot of new products out there, but Mike's team was not familiar with them and didn't feel comfortable talking about exploiting this new portfolio in front of customers. If sales didn't start to pick up, cuts would be inevitable. Mike's career wasn't just stalling, it was in danger of nose-diving.

Solution Mike sought out a software partner and developed a tool that would match customer applications with products from the new portfolio. Using the lure of a larger group contract, he was able to secure the tool on a minimal budget. He partnered also with key players from marketing to identify end-user applications and populate the system. Most importantly, once the tool was up and running, Mike worked with HR and his sales team to integrate client-facing use of the tool into each sales call. He then also initiated an internal publicity campaign to show the success of early users. Sales rose, but, more importantly, so did Mike's profile, resulting in a promotion to manager of a pan-European new products sales team.

Learning Tools can be very powerful for structuring creative activity as they harness energy and give a best practice template. It is unlikely that a tool, no matter how good, will deliver success on its own – drilling the team in the 'how' and the 'why' of the tool is vital. By acting differently and inventing a new way of working, Mike delivered a step-change in performance and was able to give his career a kick-start.

How do I maintain a good balance?

Before going out and investing in the latest and greatest software packages and tools, remember that technology is just an enabler. Success will ultimately depend on your ability to lead others, your behaviours and how you interact with them.

Be wary of being drawn into new technology too quickly. Instead, let someone else make the mistakes, but then learn quickly. If you are going to be the 'early adopter', pilot the solution (on a small scale and at minimal cost) and roll out a tried and tested working system.

If the business is adopting new technology, try to be part of the development team. Make sure that the solution is designed with your needs as a user at the forefront. If you can't do this, work with the system but log areas of underperformance and review it systematically with the implementation team. If the system is harming your performance, don't just sit there, complain.

STOP – THINK – ACT

Technology can be a daunting or exciting part of the modern manager's role, depending on your viewpoint. Think now about the technological aspects of your area of responsibility – technology that you have, technology you are obliged to work with and technological support you would like to have – then answer the following questions. Please note that this exercise may well benefit from the input of your team.

Where should we focus?	Which elements of our business could benefit from a level of automation? Focus on high-value/time-consuming processes and activities
What should we do?	What technologies are available that will help to improve these areas? Look at existing and bespoke technology developments
What benefits will we achieve	In what measurable way will the technology improve the status quo? Develop clear objectives relating to the technology and set easily reviewable KPIs

Who do we need to involve?	Who would benefit and why? Think about users and internal/external stakeholders
What resources will we require?	What level of investment would be required? Low-risk/low-cost options are preferable and go for pilot systems to prove value before the risk of a full roll-out
What is the timing?	When would be a good time to introduce the new technology? Look for a window of opportunity, such as after year-end or after annual reviews

Visit **www.Fast-Track-Me.com** to use the Fast Track online planning tool.

Virtual leadership – a strategic imperative

Ms Veronique Bourée IBM

Ms Veronique Bourée IBM

If you had to decide today what leadership competencies to assess your leaders on, what would they be? Would you refer to the charismatic leader who always seems to brighten everybody's day or would you choose the highly disciplined, but slightly coercive, sales manager whose impressive sales figures have your head spinning? Surely both profiles have admirable qualities. How relevant, though, is charisma when you are not visible to your employees? How effective is a coercive leader when there are no employees to shout at?

The new reality is that, as technology continues to grow at an exponential rate (Kurzweil) and the workforce becomes more and more mobile, organisations are becoming more virtual. Employees are online instead of behind their desks, sharing and exchanging knowledge in globally accessible databases and meeting in virtual conference rooms for chats, not the boardroom on the third floor. Who's leading them? Well, it certainly isn't Mr Charisma or Mrs Coersive!

To deal with your organisation becoming more and more virtual, you'd better find a way to assess your leaders on their virtual leadership competencies. These are not so different from those we know today, but what's important to grasp is that the relative importance of those behaviours

EXPERT VOICE

shifts and transforms in a virtual world and you need to understand which ones are important for you.

To guide you in your virtual quest, you can find a stronghold in the online gaming world. Apart from the sophisticated technology that makes any social software technology envious, this is a world that has an abundance of leadership characteristics. The best part? It's all voluntary, intrinsically driven and easily accessible. All you have to do is design your virtual organisation like an online game and create lots of interdependence, risky scenarios and empower everybody to make as many mistakes as they like to get it right and human nature will take care of the rest.

Within the online gaming world (specifically the genre massively multiplayer online role-playing game, or, MMORPG), large numbers of players interact daily with one another. They assume fictional characters, take on different roles and interact in a variety of dynamic scenarios. Even when the gamers are away from the game, the game continues to evolve and develop, thus creating an environment characterised by continuous change. Within these hybrid environments, leadership is voluntary and rotational, depending on the situation and skills required. Leaders recruit workforces across the globe and organise them to take on different challenges, develop skills and stimulate collaboration. Sound familiar?

If you're still in doubt, rest assured that this type of gaming involves complex, context-dependent, goal-directed activity and the behaviours of these gamers are worth learning from. Indeed, some studies have already been conducted.

Research so far has shown that almost all leadership behaviours encountered today in large companies are also found in online gaming. So, based on that assumption, which virtual competencies are especially relevant in a virtual world? Well, you can feel assured that you are already familiar with them, but you just have to look at them in a different light. Some of the most important virtual leadership competencies include strategic risk-taking, collaborative influence, earning trust and embracing challenge. All familiar, but here comes the shift.

Let's take trust. Most academics and management gurus will have us believe that trust is *the key* to successful leadership and if we don't spend considerable face-to-face time with our employees, we will have very little success in attaining trust.

From online gaming, we learn that trust is very important, but, what's different is that effective leaders establish trust *virtually*, based primarily on their skills, capability and knowledge. Trust is not given at face value, nor goodwill, nor favouritism. In fact, it is the perceived collective trust of the gamers in the *capability* of the leader that establishes trust.

It is not just the abundant leadership skills that can be observed in an online gaming world that are interesting but also the shifting nature of leadership all together and the implications it could have on the formal organisation as we know it today. Essentially, you can rid yourself of organisation charts and forego the effort of establishing dotted management lines. When leadership becomes voluntary, rotational and based on the collective trust and effort of the group, all that's left is creating the right environment for such behaviours to flourish.

This may seem like organisational utopia and, yes, it once was. Many factors, however, such as growing technological capability, globalisation, shifting demographics, mobilisation and so on, are all trends coming together now and they are bringing with them the possibility of a new reality and that reality is virtual.

So, you might want to get in the game yourself and arm yourself with a virtual sword. As you guide your character through a continuously changing world and find yourself struggling to align the right players to your quest, you might just realise that virtual leadership skills are no longer a nice to have but a strategic imperative for your company's survival.

EXPERT VOICE

5

IMPLEMENTING CHANGE

When you start a new management role, you will face a number of interesting challenges and opportunities, ranging from making a quick impact to getting to know the personalities involved. You will almost certainly need to make changes to the operation you have taken over. Be aware that, while these changes should be primarily motivated by a need to improve performance, you may also need to be seen to be changing things by your team and by your peers and seniors.

The challenge you face as an agent of change is inertia. Many people in their jobs are comfortable with the status quo and relatively few people embrace change as an exciting opportunity. Moving your team to the vision you have for them will take pushing, pulling, cajoling and an inspiring vision, among other things. You'll find plenty on the bookshelves about change because change is difficult to achieve. In fact, *Fortune* magazine calculated that the main reason for CEOs losing their jobs was the inability to realise change in their organisations.

Change is not impossible, however. Follow the relatively simple steps outlined in this chapter and you'll have a good chance of success.

Identify the gap

When you plan to make significant changes to the working environment and processes that you control, make sure you have understood the gap between where the operation is now and where you want it to be. This will help you to sell the change to those in your team and others.

→ Understand specific items that need to be changed.

→ Set clear goals for the unit.

→ Focus on the elements that should be measured to demonstrate the success of the change.

→ Communicate your intent and the gulf that needs to be crossed.

→ Demonstrate the problems you face and the opportunities that could be gained.

To do a 'gap analysis', you must have an idea of what the best example of this type of operation looks like – a best practice operation. Make sure that your best practice example sets out clear and objective standards, such as performance measures and statements of activity and behaviour. You can generate this by:

→ benchmarking (comparing) what you do against existing best practice operations – companies running similar but non-competing processes may be happy to show you how they work or you may be able to glean useful information from the internet

→ drawing on your experience of operations that run better

→ developing your own standard of excellence – you may find it useful and motivating to include your team in this process and it will be important to understand what your manager expects.

Let us look at an example of this.

A colleague in the soft drinks industry – let's call her Jane – was anxious to make a mark when she was appointed Marketing Strategy Director. She was aware that there were several opportunities to make improvements in how the business organised and delivered marketing projects, but she needed to make a clear case for this by comparing her organisation with a best practice benchmark one. She had worked for other similar businesses and took the time to talk to external experts who had views on what the best companies were doing and also what future best practice might look like. Jane put together a picture of all the elements that made up her view of best practice and used a model exactly like the organisational effectiveness audit – the first tool in the Directors' toolkit, on page 205.

Now go out and measure the performance of your own operation. Here are some of the ways in which you can do this.

→ **Look at performance in terms of numbers** What measures do you have in place already (examples might be efficiency, sales, profit, costs, customer satisfaction, job turnover)? What else can you measure (to compare to a benchmark)?

→ **Talk to your team, internal and external customers and senior stakeholders** How do they perceive your performance? What examples do they have of good and bad practices?

→ **Look hard at the business process** Make a chart of what happens sequentially in the process. Does it all make sense or are there places where the process loops, steps are repeated or communication seems inefficient?

You now have a good understanding – perhaps at high level at this stage – of the gap you now hope to bridge, the difference between the results of your survey and the standard of excellence to which you aspire.

To continue with our example, Jane collated figures on the number of existing projects and the success rate of historical projects. She also interviewed senior managers and brand managers to understand their viewpoints. She compared her analysis against the benchmark. In her report, she highlighted the fact that projects were given resources on a subjective basis, senior managers were frustrated because they had little idea of what projects were underway and the brand managers had no transparency regarding why their projects were approved or not.

Finally, she highlighted in her executive summary the degree to which resources across the business were being wasted, but, most importantly, that there was a significant risk of the organisation being overtaken by much more efficient competitors. This created a real sense of urgency.

Create urgency

To get your team to change (and others to accept that you need to change), you must create a sense of urgency. People must see that it is no longer acceptable to stay as you are, that there is a 'burning platform' from which you must move if you are not to be overtaken by the competition. This is not necessarily easy to do, but is essential if you are to establish any momentum for your change.

To do this, you need to take the following steps.

→ Communicate (report, present, do a web-cast – whatever will have the highest impact) the need for change to all those who matter. If you write a report, use an executive summary to highlight the key points, but also include *all* your data to show that you have done extensive research to support your views. Use diagrams and performance figures that spotlight significant areas of poor performance, wastage and discrepancies against your competition.

→ Regularly discuss the issues behind the need for change with all those whose support you need and haven't yet won over. These conversations need to be one on one and you must both promote your views and listen to and understand the concerns of the other person. If you are to have any chance of effecting change, you will need the support of at least 20 per cent of the senior stakeholders.

→ Make the need to change the headline in all your meetings and in other meetings where you have an opportunity to raise it.

Bear in mind that people don't necessarily like bad news so they may defend the status quo. You will have to push against this and deal with other detractors who may not want to listen to your message.

'Switching off' the old system is the classic way to engender a level of urgency. If your stakeholders know that in three months the old mechanism will no longer be available to them, they will more readily move over to the new one. The panic raised by the prospect of systems crashing when the world's computer clocks changed over to one minute past midnight on 31 December 1999 caused a huge amount of change, all of which had to be completed by that deadline.

Returning to our example, with significant risks evident, Jane very quickly had the ear of the managing director and used this to good effect, ensuring that he influenced all those around him and started to question the current approach.

Plan

Making a plan will drive delivery of anything significant and executing change is no exception.

The first step in planning for change is to build a vision for where you want to be at the end of this particular initiative. If it is appropriate (doesn't have a negative impact on those involved), it will be useful to get your immediate management team involved in this process. It helps to get them to buy into the end result and the journey. Moreover, they will probably have useful inputs. The vision and objectives should ideally be SMART (see page 48) to make them clear and allow you to monitor progress against them.

Planning needn't be complex – a simple plan is easier to do, easier to implement and easier to control. The table gives you an example of Jane's simple change project plan.

Finally, spend some time thinking about risks. Work with your project team or perhaps some of the stakeholders that you have identified as key affected people. They will have interesting ideas for what might go wrong and will also come up with approaches for mitigating or resolving them.

QUICK TIP *BE A GOOD PROJECT MANAGER*
Even strategic projects are governed by **time**, **cost** and **performance**. Use a good project management structure to deliver your goals effectively.

Milestones	Deadline	Details	Responsibility
Stakeholder support managed	End March	Run a stakeholder analysis Conduct stakeholder interviews Set up communication plan	Jane
New marketing project management process designed	End April	Design team put together (involve end-users) Design sessions run Outputs communicated to key stakeholders	Jane and brand managers
Pilot web-tool configured and set up for use	Mid-April	Software vendor chosen Objectives and needs established Tool configured and refined with end-users	Jane and software supplier
Project manager training completed	End April	Training provider chosen and briefed Training completed	Jane and training provider
Senior managers' meeting reconfigured	End April	Pilot tool partially loaded Senior managers briefed on changes and pilot meeting run Use feedback to review	Jane
All projects loaded on to web-tool	End May		Project managers and software administrator
Communication managed	End May	Communication plan built Stakeholder communication delivered Broader business communication delivered	Jane
Handover completed	End June	Agree changes in responsibility Software management handed over to IT Senior managers committed to new process	Jane

Build support

Implementing change successfully requires the support of all those who can influence the output of the change – we call them stakeholders. In the end, successful change is about getting people to do things differently and all sorts of people will have an interest in either advancing or resisting change.

To build support among your stakeholders, first identify and list all the people who have a role to play in the changes. They could be any of the following.

→ **Those directly affected by the changes you have planned.** You will need to make sure that this group of people adopts the new ways of operating and are persuaded to move away from the old way, which may be reassuring because of its familiarity. This group of people will have a big impact on the success of your change. You should build a communication plan for this group that motivates and persuades them to adopt your changes and move away from their default behaviour and the status quo. You should also regularly consult with these people – either as a group or as individuals – and talk through your vision and the associated benefits. You could do this in a presentation style initially, but you will need to use an interactive style later on so that you can bring to the surface their concerns and issues and deal with them. You might also consider involving this group in the change-planning process – the more involved they can be in developing the vision and the specific changes, the more likely they are to adopt and work with the new approach.

→ **Those indirectly affected.** Other functions in the business who work with your team or support your team (like HR and IT) may need to understand the impact of the changes so that they can effect a seamless transition. In some situations you may need to include customers in this category. If you think customers will potentially be adversely affected by any disruption associated with the change activity, you should first think about how this can be avoided and what you can do during the change process to mitigate any impact on them. If this is not feasible, you must communicate with customers, ask for their patience during the transition, remembering to sell your vision of the future. It may be tough to do this, but, if you don't, the customers may go somewhere else.

→ **Sponsors and senior influencers.** Senior managers will be able to influence the outcome of your project to a greater degree than anyone else and you should do your best to keep these people on your side. They may be responsible for funding your changes, be affected by your changes or see your changes as a threat to their domain, vision and so on. Draw up a list of these individuals – there probably won't be more than ten – and work out which of them will support you and which might resist. Develop a plan to work with your supporters, getting them to influence their peers and talk positively about your project. Engage the resisters by trying to win them over to your vision and showing how your vision will help them meet their objectives. If they don't become, at least, impartial, work out how you can manage to deliver your plans without their support.

Here is an example of Jane's stakeholder analysis.

Stakeholder	Influence	Support (−5 – +5)	Action
Tom, managing director	High	+5	Exploit Tom's support – get him to raise the subject at monthly briefings, promote it with senior managers
Alan, operations director	High/medium	+2	Understand any objections and manage
James, finance director	High/medium	−3	Concerned about costs and links to new ERP – work to reduce his concerns
Charlotte, marketing director	High/medium	+2	Likes idea of more visibility, but slightly concerned about impact on brand managers – involve her in design process
Marketing managers	Medium	−4	Concerned that this will erode their decision-making power – involve them in the design process and ensure they retain power where appropriate
Brand managers	Medium	−2	Worried about extra work – get them to work on design of new templates so that work levels are reduced
IT	Low	0	
R&D	Low	0	

CASE STORY *CHANGE FROM WITHIN, DAVE'S STORY*

Narrator Dave had been with the organisation for 15 years. He had moved steadily through the management hierarchy, but was frustrated that his influence and impact were on the wane. Moreover, he could see some big issues that needed to be addressed. How could he deliver what the business needed and re-energise his career? He needed to up his game.

Context This multi-billion dollar global player had a great track record of success. The business was renowned for its marketing skills, backed up by a powerful and respected R&D function that continued to deliver cutting-edge products

Issue The business was having to come to terms with a new market paradigm. There was a need to build customer marketing capability as well as address the traditional end-user. The business recognised this challenge, but actually acting on it and delivering a change in focus was proving difficult – nobody seemed to have a realistic plan.

Solution Tough as it was, Dave stepped away from the operational numbers game everybody seemed so preoccupied with. He mapped out the critical issues required to engage effectively with new customers. He took some small risks in getting a pilot off the ground, working with a few colleagues and securing some experienced external resource. He then married the results with his vision to sell a simple, ongoing execution plan to senior management.

Learning Big business can be seen as hard to change from within and at a mid-level position, but nothing could be further from the truth. You *can* get out of rut – if you have a plan. Setting a vision and simple plan requires the ability to step back from the business. Delivering a short-term 'small' result will help secure buy-in for the broader strategy.

 QUICK TIP **BREVITY**

Keep your action plan on one page – most managers don't have the time or attention span to read more than one page, so get the key points on to a single-page executive summary. Supplement it with details, to show that you have done good work and for the implementers, who will need them.

Keep it on track

Giving your initiative a good launch is important if it is to go well. All projects need regular inputs of energy, though, so it is vital that you monitor the progress of the initiative relentlessly. This achieves at least two things:

→ it makes sure that the project activities are kept on track and gives you the confidence that all is going to plan (or can be rectified if not)

→ it demonstrates to all others that this is important to you and the business and you will do what it takes to see this through.

Others will begin to understand that this is not just another 'here today, gone tomorrow' initiative, but a genuine plan to be seen through to its conclusion.

You can monitor progress very simply:

→ check that the activities in your plan are being done to schedule

→ hold people to their commitments – make sure that they do what they say they will

→ keep an eye on your vision and objectives and check that the work being done will still take you there

→ at each stage, think about what could go wrong in the next stage and what you can do to prevent it being an issue.

You will sometimes find yourself in a position where people are not doing what they have committed to, so, to keep your change process on track, you will need to find out why this is happening. For help on this, see under Managing Poor Performance, page 94.

Communicate success

When you are changing aspects of your team or business, you can re-energise people by occasionally focusing on success.

In the early stages, you may have to look hard for 'wins', but it pays to identify success in, for example, the achievement of a significant milestone, activity of a team and, best of all, a positive shift in your overall metrics. For instance, if you have been changing the way you work with customers, it will be worth publicising the fact that you have made a small but sustained improvement in customer satisfaction figures. This shows all stakeholders that your changes are having an effect.

In some situations, you may be able to plan things so that 'quick wins' become apparent more easily. To continue the example, if customer satisfaction changes are going to take a while to emerge, you may be able to point to the completion of customer relationship training as a 'quick win' on the road to your vision. To ensure this selling of success does not get forgotten, build and highlight the likely 'quick wins' into your plan and determine in advance how such successes will be communicated. For example, if you have a corporate event, get the project on the agenda and make sure that you have some good news to tell people.

QUICK TIP *COMMUNICATE STRATEGIC PROGRESS*
Tell other functions what you have changed so that they can align themselves to capitalise on your new strategy. Don't assume that they will know what you have achieved and what this means to them.

At some point in the process, you may be able to demonstrate that your changes have started to take root and people are beginning to regard the new way as the norm. This is particularly important if you are involved in moving people away from an existing approach.

Beware, however. Quick wins are worth celebrating, but they are not the end point. If you report too many small successes that *aren't* affecting the overall performance you are trying to change, people may become cynical. Worse is to report on an improvement that you are not sure will be sustained. If the measure falls back again the next time you measure it, you will lose credibility.

QUICK TIP **CELEBRATE OTHERS' SUCCESSES**
You are part of a team so your co-managers are on the same side. When they achieve outstanding results, your congratulations will be appreciated, whether by email, phone or over a coffee.

Sustain the momentum – make excellence part of business-as-usual

All your good work changing the operations you are involved with must at some stage become the normal way to work.

During the period of change, people will be worried, excited, resistant and talking. If you've done the job well so far, the new approach will be high on their agenda. Your job is not complete, however, until they cease to talk about it as a new thing and, instead, it is merely the way things are – and, if you're lucky, 'Here's how we can make it even better.'

The best way for you to approach this is to make the change operational rather than a project. As the change programme draws to a close, start to move away from project meetings and review your new ways of working in your normal management meetings. Make sure that you are reviewing new or relevant metrics that focus people on how this new approach is running and remove any measures that take the focus back to the old way of doing things. Use the meetings to start a 'continuous improvement' mindset for the new system. What can be done to improve it? How can we further lift the performance measures?

These activities will help to build the changes into the fabric of the business and embed your good vision as a business norm. There are some other things you can do to sustain the change, too.

→ Align the appraisal and reward structures with the new ways of working. You must ensure that everybody with a role in the new approach is rewarded for making that new way work well. Rewards may come as financial bonuses, but could equally be public recognition and personal gratitude and encouragement.

→ Sometimes there will be an old process or system that your change has replaced or upgraded. You should dismantle any remnants of the old approach to make it impossible for people to revert to it.

→ Continue to communicate ongoing successes and highlight performance measures that are going in the right direction

Let's see how Jane is doing.

Jane took great care to manage this part of her change programme effectively. All the way through the implementation of the new marketing project management process, she worked hard to involve people in the change so that they would adopt the end result more readily. She ensured that senior managers now used the web-tool to review all the marketing projects live on a screen in the meeting room, to approve projects or get brand managers involved to explain things they didn't like or understand. The biggest success factor for Jane was that all financial support for projects was approved through this meeting and web-tool – if your project wasn't entered into the system, you couldn't get approval to continue. A very persuasive situation!

QUICK TIP BUDDY UP

You won't be the first or last person to find yourself in a challenging position. Are there people in similar positions at your company (maybe in different functions)? Why not hook up with them on a monthly basis for a coffee and review of strategies. Ask HR to put you in touch with people with similar experience or in a similar position.

Critical success factors

So how can we increase our chances of succeeding in implementing the change?

As you start to implement your new approach, reflect on the factors that will drive success. You can't focus on everything at once, so where do you start?

→ Focus on opportunities that are of high value and fit with the current business priorities. This tends to get everyone's attention and commitment.

→ Ensure that the senior team shows *active* commitment to your changes – after all, they will have the greatest impact on business culture and if they don't take it seriously, no one else will.

→ Create a balanced team, in terms of skills, experience and behaviours, if possible, and ensure sufficient budgetary and other resources are allocated to the overall implementation process.

→ Build your changes into business-as-usual in order to minimise the perceived workload or associated overhead. This is best done by making lots of small changes, such as modifying a meeting agenda or adding an item to a weekly checklist.

→ Install systems and tools to support the consistent application of best practice across all teams – effectively creating a 'common language'.

→ Develop skills to improve the quality of the work people do in generating ideas and project management as this will improve the overall effectiveness and efficiency of the process.

→ Reward people for adopting the changes, in non-financial ways as well as by giving them bonuses.

→ Evaluate progress and performance honestly, openly and without politics, making sure that the evidence supports your conclusions and is presented in a blame-free way.

→ Finally, communicate successes or 'quick wins' to all interested stakeholders so that people can see that the overall approach is working and worthwhile.

STOP – THINK – ACT

Implementing change in any organisation, whether a business or not, is a significant challenge and will not necessarily be quick or easy. As a manager, however, you will need to make changes to your areas of responsibility, whether that is directed by you or dictated from elsewhere in the organisation. Use the table below to identify and/or prioritise any changes that you need to make and commit to planning the change process using the stages described above.

What should we do?	What changes do we need to make in this part of the organisation? Which have the highest prioritiy?
Who do we need to involve?	Who needs to be involved in the planning of these changes and why?
What resources will we require?	What information, facilities, materials, equipment or budget will be required?
What is the timing?	When will we have a plan in place to drive these particular changes through?

Visit **www.Fast-Track-Me.com** to use the Fast Track online planning tool.

What does it take to lead change successfully?

Professor Malcolm Higgs University of Southampton, School of Management

EXPERT VOICE

There is widespread agreement that one of the biggest challenges facing organisations today is ensuring that necessary change is implemented effectively. Yet it is widely accepted that only 30 per cent of changes are successful. At the same time, it is clear that effective change implementation is one of the most important leadership roles and challenges in today's business context.

Our beliefs about leadership are often based on a leadercentric approach – leaders directing all that happens in an organisation. At the same time, many have suggested that a major cause of the endemic failure of change in organisations can be attributed to the failure of leadership. It has been suggested that the development of change leadership capability can, in itself, provide organisations in today's context with significant competitive advantage.

Change leadership behaviours

Against this background, our recent research study with an international and diverse sample drawn from 30 organisations explored the question, 'What makes change work?' The study involved interviewing leaders at all levels. They were asked to tell their stories about both successful and unsuccessful changes.

As a result of analysing around 70 such stories, 4 broad leadership behaviour sets were identified. These were then related to the relative success of the change initiatives. These key behaviours were as follows.

Attractor

→ Connects with others at an emotional level, embodies the future intent of the organisation.

→ Tunes in to day-to-day reality, sees themes and patterns that connect to a wider movement and form, which creates a compelling story for the organisation.

→ Uses this to set the context for how things fit together, working the story into the life of the organisation so that every conversation and decision 'makes sense'.

→ Visibly works beyond personal ambition to serve a higher purpose – the organisation and its wider community.

→ Is consciously aware of his or her own leadership and adapts this for a specific purpose.

Edge and tension

→ Tells it as it is – describes reality with respect, yet without compromise.

→ In times of turbulence, has constancy – does not withdraw from tough stuff and keeps people's hands in the fire.

→ Can spot and challenge assumptions – creates discomfort by challenging existing paradigms and disrupting habitual ways of doing things.

→ Sets the bar high and keeps it there, stretching the goals and limits of what is possible.

→ Does not compromise on talent – pays attention to getting and keeping top talent.

Container

→ Sets and contracts boundaries, clear expectations and hard rules so that people know what to operate on (performance expectations) and how they need to operate (values and behaviours).

→ Is self-assured, confident, takes a stand for his or her beliefs and is not anxious when challenging conditions.

→ Provides affirming and encouraging signals, creating ownership, trust and confidence.

→ Makes it 'safe' to say risky things and have the 'hard to have' conversations' via empathy and high-quality dialogue skills.

→ Creates alignment at the top to ensure consistency and constancy of approach.

Creates movement

→ Demonstrates a commitment that engenders trust, enabling the system to go to new places, learn about itself and act differently.

→ Frees people to new possibilities by making him- or herself vulnerable and open.

→ Understands what is happening in the moment and breaks established patterns and structures in ways that create movement in the here and now.

→ Powerfully enquires about ripe systemic issues to enable deep change to happen.

→ Creates time and space (including attending to its physical qualities) for transforming encounters.

In this study we found that the combination of *all four* of these practices explained around *50 per cent* of the variance in change success. Furthermore, we found that leadercentric behaviours were associated with unsuccessful change implementation.

Building on this, we examined in more detail the practices of those leaders who deployed a balance of all four of the change leadership behaviours. In doing this, we found that the differentiating behaviours were as follows.

→ **They understand and incorporate the wider change context** They lead upwards and outwards to create space for the organisation and catalyse energy for change.

→ **They build their leadership teams to think and act for the whole** They require them to step up and back to hold a bigger space and be strategic, interdependent and systemic, thereby creating an aligned, transforming energy at the top.

→ **They work on the underlying system that produces the performance outcomes** They show an intense ability to tune in to their organisation, see patterns, notice *how* things are said not just *what's* being said, identify the few key assumptions and patterns that, if shifted, would transform everything, then initiate creative moves to make those shifts.

→ **They are patient with people as they make the transition** Yet they still keep the change on course. Others, by contrast, were passive and just stood back and waited.

→ **They display extremely high levels of self-awareness** They are able to sense the impact they have on others, seek feedback and exchange on this and consciously use their presence in the organisation to create shifts (evidencing leadership).

→ **They set tangible measures for the change** They open up the system to share information and performance data to both hold up a mirror to catalyse people to take personal ownership for improving things.

Conclusions

From the above study it is evident that a leadercentric approach is counterproductive. Yet, our attempts to understand the nature of leadership have all implicitly been leadercentric. Thus, much that we have been told about effective leadership will potentially inhibit our ability to make change happen in our organisation.

If the results of this study are supported by other studies, we need to ask whether or not the questions we have been exploring in relation to leadership enable us to learn anything that will enable us to find and develop leaders able to make change happen effectively. Perhaps now is the time to forget what we *think* we know about leadership and begin to explore its role and nature in a new way.

Overall, perhaps we can conclude that, if we want to make change happen successfully, there is a need to lead less and change more. **"**

EXPERT VOICE

PART C

CAREER
FAST TRACK

Whatever you have decided to do in terms of developing your career as a manager, to be successful you need to take control, plan ahead and focus on the things that will really make a difference.

The first ten weeks of a new role will be critical. Get them right and you will be off to a flying start and probably succeed. Get them wrong and you will come under pressure and even risk being moved on rather quickly. Plan this initial period to make sure you are not overwhelmed by the inevitable mass of detail that will assail you on arrival. Make sure that other people's priorities do not put you off the course you have set yourself.

Once you have successfully eased yourself into your new role and gained the trust of your boss and the team, you can start to make things happen. First, focus on your leadership style and how it needs to change to suit the new role; then focus on the team. Are they the right people, and if so, what will make them work more effectively as a team?

Finally, at the appropriate time, you need to think about your next career move and whether you are interested in getting to the top and becoming a company director. It is not for everyone, as the commitment, time and associated stress can be offputting, but the sense of responsibility and leadership can be enormously rewarding.

You've concentrated on performance up until now – now it's time to look at your Fast Track career.

THE FIRST TEN WEEKS

The first ten weeks of starting a new role in management are probably the most critical – get them wrong and you risk failure; get them right and you will enjoy and thrive in your new role. What do you need to do, where should you focus, and what must you avoid at all costs?

The Fast Track manager, in order to the take control in a new role, will seek to understand key facts, build relationships and develop simple mechanisms for monitoring and control, establishing simple but effective team processes. This task can be simplified by using modern technology so it becomes effortless and part of day-to-day behaviour.

Changing roles

Why is this a critical time?

Whenever you start a new role or job, whether within your existing business or joining a new company, you have an opportunity to make a positive impression on others. In fact, you'll have something of a 'honeymoon' period, in which you are regarded as the smart new kid on the block who might make a real impact and get things moving. Recognise, however, that you will only have one chance to make a first impression[1]

1 Watkins, M. (2000) *The First 90 Days*. Boston, MA: Harvard Business School Press.

– get the first few months wrong and it could impact your relationships with others for a very long time.

During a period of transition, the team you are joining will normally have few preconceptions about you. People will typically have an open mind and be willing to try new ideas, giving you the benefit of the doubt. We often see this phenomenon when consultants are called in to resolve a critical business issue. The consultants often say exactly the same things as some of the internal managers, but, as outsiders, their views are respected and acted on.

The first ten weeks are typically a period of high emotional energy, when activities will often get a higher level of enthusiasm and commitment than usual. Use this time wisely and you will gain significant advantage.

What are the potential pitfalls?

While this period of transition presents opportunities to make a good impression, take care not to get it wrong. Few people recover from a bad start in a new role. You will be faced with a number of challenges to overcome.

→ **You will lack knowledge and expertise in your new role.** This will make you vulnerable to making wrong decisions.

→ **Getting in with the wrong people can limit your opportunities for future promotion.** In every team there will be a mixture of people and opinions, so try to understand the office politics before you join the team or department.

→ **There will be a lot to do in a short period of time and you may well feel overwhelmed by it all.**

→ **Most effective managers rely heavily on their informal networks, but, in the early stages of a new job, these don't exist.**

→ **It is tempting to try to do too much too quickly.** It will take time to assimilate information and form your vision. If you try to do too much in the first couple of weeks, you will probably get things wrong and rapidly lose credibility.

What is the worst-case scenario?

Because people often give the benefit of the doubt to those who are starting a new job or joining a new team, things often go well for a period of time. If you make mistakes they will forgive you because you're new to the job. This is what is meant by the 'honeymoon period'. New football coaches, for example, are allowed to lose the first few games without too much criticism. After a period of time (the first ten weeks), however, you, like the coaches, will need to perform well, meeting the expectations of key stakeholders and winning them over as supporters.

During this initial period, it is vital that you take the necessary steps to set yourself up for longer-term success. Otherwise, you run the risk of, as it were, falling into the chasm – you make a good start, but then people start to see what you are doing as just another management initiative. Plan your first ten weeks carefully in order to set yourself up for longer-term success.

QUICK TIP *TOMORROW IS ANOTHER DAY*
Don't get bogged down or lose focus because of yesterday's successes or failures. Use a 'to do' list to kick-start each day. Be flexible, depending on what happened, but make sure that you are moving forwards according to a set plan.

The first ten weeks

What should I do before I start?

At the end of the first ten weeks in your new role, you will invariably say, 'I wish I'd known at the start all that I know now!' In the first ten weeks, you will assimilate so much information and knowledge about the business, your team, your function, the processes, the people, the stakeholders and so on that your ability to make decisions and plan will get rapidly stronger as time passes. Without rushing things, however, you do want to at least give the impression of hitting the ground running. So, before starting a new job, do your research.

→ What will it entail?

→ What opportunities are there in this sector, process or business?

→ What is the competition doing?

→ What might success look like?

→ Who are the key people I will need to get to know, both internally and externally (the internet may help here)? Who are the experts?

→ Where are the likely weaknesses and how can I develop quick wins from these?

→ What could go wrong and what could I do to prevent or miti-gate those issues?

Think also about your own strengths and weaknesses. What have you learned from your previous role or from analytical exercises such as per-sonality profiles? How will others see you?

From this information, start to think about how you yourself will need to change. How will you behave differently, what knowledge will you need to gain and what new skills would be useful? Understanding these things will help to build your confidence.

What will the first ten weeks look like?

Use the following suggestions to put together a plan for your first ten weeks in your new position. While you will get into the detail of each area in your first ten weeks, recognise that you may be able to make a start before you take the job or start in your new role.

Week 1: Meet, greet and observe

The first week will be different in different situations. If you're starting a new role in a new company, all sorts of induction activities and meetings may be organised for you. If it's a new role in your existing company, this probably won't be organised, but it's still important. Make sure that you arrange to meet all the key stakeholders for your new role. These will typically include your boss, senior managers (boss's boss level), work colleagues, your team, functional heads, experts, customers and suppliers. Do a stakeholder analysis and think about the influence of each of these people, their likely impacts on your success and how they might like to be communicated with. Here is an example of such an analysis.

Stakeholder	Needs	Influence (1–10)	Support (–5 – +5)	Communication plan
Tom Yates, finance director	Positive about my role Wants to see results soon	10	+4	Develop plan for delivering genuine quick wins and share long-term vision
Ann Marshall, marketing colleague	Big influence on my department and keen to help	7	+2	Keep on side with view of long-term vision
Antonio Coplo, purchasing	Could have an impact on some of my team and seems uninterested	5	–1	Find out his objectives and work out how I can help him deliver
Mark Foster, supply chain	Seems to see us as competitors, but his influence and likely impact are low	2	–2	Attempt to build relationship, but don't commit much time
James Dingle, key customer	His feedback will be critical to my success, but don't yet know where he stands	7	0	Set up meetings to understand needs and develop relationship – share vision and quick wins
Customer service reps	Members of my team who will need to change how they operate – they probably won't like change	6	–5	Share top-line vision, but get them to develop the detail of what that means to them and how change might be of benefit – be clear about the dangers of *not* changing

Customers often provide the best insights for improving a business, so make sure that you listen carefully to what they have to say. Start to think about how it will influence your area of responsibility. Also, start to build relationships with your key customers and set things up so that you can come back to them at a later date to talk about progress.

Do not go into initial meetings or telephone conversations without stopping and thinking them through.

→ What is the impression you want to give and what do you need to do to make sure this will happen?

→ Think about what could go wrong and what you can do to make sure risks are avoided or mitigated.

→ Make sure that initial conversations focus on them, not you. Take time to really understand what their agenda is, what their concerns are and what their ideas are for the future.

→ Try not to state your ideas at the initial meeting – it is much better just to listen hard. Indeed, it is often said that influence most belongs to the person who says least during the meeting, but provides the summary at the end and proposes the action plan.

→ You'll probably be asked for your views or plans or similar, so be prepared with some answers – nothing too controversial or that will tie you down in the future.

Finally, make sure that you achieve a good handover from your predecessor. There may be a number of factors at play here (the person may have been successful and is being promoted or have been in this role for years and made little progress) that means he or she will be more or less disposed to talk to you. Whatever the case, do what you can to extract all the information you can about the team, stakeholders, pitfalls and critical parts of the process you'll be involved in. It is also vital to remember that this is your predecessor's view and perception – make sure you don't slip into the same mould without thinking analytically about what you have been told.

Week 2: Understand the business

Depending on where you have come from, you will need to spend more or less time getting to understand how this business ticks.

→ What drives the business – customers, sales or profit, something else?

→ What performance measures are they using at the top level? What's the vision and/or strategy? What are this year's targets?

→ Sometimes in a business you can identify where the critical added value lies. It might be that it is a great innovator or good at predicting the future value of its products or can find the best-value ingredients or components. All this analysis will help you to build a picture of the business.

You will have a good idea of what's going on as a result of your stake-holder meetings, but you may now benefit from talking with others who may be closer to understanding the business drivers. Finance would be a good place to start. What is being reported on a regular basis and which bits of the reports are acted on in meetings? See if you can attend meetings that may be peripheral to your area of responsibility but may give you a sense of the business's priorities and the culture that exists within which you will have to work.

Next, start to translate what you have learned into what it means for your part of the business – your function and team. If your boss has clear objectives for you (often he or she won't!), clarify them. Whatever the situation, find out how your *boss* is being measured. What are his or her objectives and which ones can you impact? Where is he or she struggling and in need of help?

You may also start to glean indications of the scope of your role and what senior people see as the limits you must work within. You may choose to ignore these limits if the opportunities are good, but beware stepping on the toes of senior stakeholders – they can have a very nega-tive impact on your career if they are influential and feel threatened by you.

As the new boss, you will be involved in all sorts of activity immedi-ately: you may be taking over the chair at a number of meetings and asked to make decisions. Don't rush into changes at this stage, even though you may be tempted by some apparently glaring opportuni-ties. Use this time to observe what's going on and how people behave. Think about the meetings you're running or attending. Do they need to happen? Could they be run better? What are the objectives?

Watch how people go about their work. Does it look organised and professional or can you see duplications, wasted effort and inefficien-cies? Start building a list and generating ideas for improvements. This list will be iterative, so develop your ideas and test them over the next few days or weeks. That way you will be able to refine how you can start to make changes. You are starting to assess opportunities for making 'quick wins' in the early part of your new tenure.

Your quick snapshot of the business should also confirm what budgets and resources you have and how it has changed from previous years. This will help you to assess the level of importance the business places on this topic. Use the checklist at the end of this chapter to check that you have the information you need.

Week 3: Secure quick wins

Those watching your progress in your new role are expecting you to make a difference. It may be unfair, but some will be looking for signs of a change already, in Week 3. You may actually be ready to make some quick changes, but it is important at this stage that, whatever you do, it is seen to be positive and effective.

Start to list and categorise the changes you plan to make in the short term. If you're lucky, you will have identified one or two changes that will significantly impact the business, improving efficiency or perhaps changing the way customers view the business. It's unusual at this stage to find these opportunities, but, by digging carefully, you may come up with some ideas. For example, your team members may have been suppressed over the years and be delighted to contribute or your boss may be only too happy to help you succeed. In the latter case, remember, he or she appointed you and will want to demonstrate the wisdom of that choice.

It is more likely that your ideas for early changes will revolve around data flows, decision-making and other such activities. Here are some typical places to look to make improvements.

→ Meetings – are any unnecessary, poorly run or planned?

→ Reports – are you getting the information you need or could the information be presented better?

→ Are there obvious conflicts in the way your team members interact with others that cause inefficiencies?

→ Can you make any quick changes to approval processes to speed things up? Are there approvals missing that, if introduced, will reduce errors and poor decisions?

Changes of this nature can lift the heads of the people in your area of responsibility, showing them that you are in charge and intend to make things happen. Doing this will also demonstrate to others that you are already figuring out ways to improve things.

Make a list of your ideas for change as you progress into Week 3, then prioritise them in terms of their impact on the business and urgency. Measure 'impact' in terms of how each change will support a specific business imperative or the difference it will make to overall profitability. Measure 'urgency' in terms of specific deadlines that need to be met or windows of opportunity, such as a shut-down during the summer holiday period.

Then, for those changes that you consider a priority, identify one or two you know you can implement quickly, within a few days, with little risk. Don't take too many risks at this stage – you may want to make an early impression, but not the wrong one!

Think carefully about potential problems and take time to meet with the relevant stakeholders to ensure fast success. You can then communicate these quick wins in a way that builds commitment and your credibility. Reflect on the impact on not just senior stakeholders but also those in your team. If you're dressing up something to make it look good to those outside your area, your people will see through it immediately and not be impressed. Damage to your credibility of this type at this stage will have a serious impact on your ability to steer your team through future changes.

There will be other changes that take longer to implement, but still qualify as quick wins if you can deliver them within your honeymoon period. This is a good time to involve members of your team. Talk them through or steer them towards the opportunities you have identified (or *they* may have identified when asked). Give them short-term objectives to resolve the issues and coach them through the planning and change management that may be required.

For example, one of your team may come to you and say that there is a problem with the systems and software they are using. It's something that she has been concerned about for a while but has never been fixed. Give her guidelines on analysing the situation, thinking of solutions and how to involve IT. Ask her to come back to you with some options for fixing the problem that might cover a range of prices and time frames. Both she and you want to make a quick impact here, so try to find an affordable solution that can be implemented within a few weeks. Then, with your coaching and support, if she needs it, get her to project manage the implementation and the changes to team practices. This will build a strong and appropriate relationship with your team members and help you deliver early results.

Week 4: Conduct a SWOT analysis

Critically evaluate each aspect of your areas of responsibility – processes, people and so on. Identify those areas that you consider to be strengths and weaknesses, and then those reflecting opportunities and threats. Make a quick list, but then sift through and prioritise it down to the top five in each category. Use the management self-assessment given in Chapter 2.

If you conduct this on your own, recognise that it will reflect your first impressions, so some of your conclusions will be valid while others may be incorrect. Take time to validate your thoughts with your boss and other key stakeholders – this will provide an opportunity to get to know them better and start thinking about ways to address weaknesses and exploit strengths. Of course, your team members may well have valuable contributions to make to this, so it may pay to get them involved. Watch, though, for any internal competition and conflict that may be skewing their opinions. Here's an example of a completed SWOT.

Strengths	Weaknesses
There are some strong and capable individuals in the team Individual problem solving is well done There is good technical expertise in the group	The working processes and practices are poorly defined and, consequently, controls are not good Some of the individuals have been in place a long time and may be set in their ways The department is poorly regarded by those outside Teamwork is non-existent and, as a result of poor leadership, individuals act on their own without regard to others

Opportunities	Threats
There is great support from my local line manager and from the managing director of the business There are significant areas for quick improvements to how the business operates Customer pressures on the overall business will justify investment in this function	Taking on too many projects may exceed the resources available Other functions tend to take a competitive position and will not be forgiving of any mistakes

This team leader has identified some key strengths on which he can build and some good opportunities that will help him develop his function as he would like. Meanwhile, there are some significant weaknesses to be overcome, as well as a few threats from outside. On balance, this SWOT gives the team leader the opportunity to focus his priorities.

You will also need to conduct an appraisal of your team. At this stage, this will probably just mean those who report to you. Do a SWOT analysis for each individual and start to think about the organisational structure that you have inherited. What do you think your future structure might look like and how do you see your current team fitting into that?

Where you (or perhaps your boss or stakeholders) have identified an issue – someone who doesn't appear to be performing well – start to think about ways to manage the situation. As you develop your vision for the future, which of your team members do you see as champions who will help you get there, and who will hinder progress or even block the way? Start thinking about your options for managing this situation.

 CASE STORY PERFORMANCE MANAGEMENT, WILLIAM'S STORY

Narrator William was running a data centre for a leading telephony organisation. He had asked for the job – one that had more or less ended the careers of the last two incumbents.

Context The business supplied telephone and data services to business clients in Europe and North America. Flexible service and reliability had been the cornerstones of its major growth and this was built on a state-of-the-art IT infrastructure.

Issue The IT infrastructure was beginning to creak as the business grew fast. More applications were being launched on a regular basis and the IT support service had been outsourced to India. Agreements on service levels were not being met and problems weren't being eradicated. There was a sticking-plaster culture that simply meant problems recurred on a regular basis – costing time, money and reputation.

Solution A key initiative involved the creation of an integrated approach to root cause analysis. It also included the identification of roles and responsibilities for root cause champions. As well as establishing ownership, William saw to it that all key staff in Europe and India were trained in root cause analysis and given simple tools to capture and share data. Finally, William introduced a new metric – 'percentage of problems traced to root cause'. It was the key metric at weekly management meetings and was incorporated in the annual review for key managers. This figure started at 11 per cent and rose to over 90 per cent in under 18 months. The business was able to remedy system errors once and for all and take on new applications, helping the business to grow.

Learning Ownership and mechanics will drive performance, but systematic management of all people around a single strategic metric is the most effective way to change results.

Week 5: Create a vision

At the end of your first month in your new role, stop and take stock of where you are. Reflect on what you have learned and the key messages you have received from your boss and other key stakeholders. You should now have enough information and insights to put together your vision for the team for the next two to three years.

Start at the end and think about what you want to have achieved before you move on to your next role, whether it be in six months or three years. The clearer your vision of what success will look like, the more likely it is that you will achieve it. You will make it completely clear if you can attach numbers to your vision. Depending on the function you are running, these numbers could be the amount or percentage of profit, sales overall or customer satisfaction or one of the various efficiency measures and ratios. Think about how you want people to remember you after you have moved on. What will they say about you?

Then, translate this vision into a team strategy or plan. This should clarify what you will do in terms of the products and services the company provides and, perhaps just as importantly, what you're not going to do. Clarifying boundaries helps to focus the team and ensure that your limited resources and budget are not spread too thinly. How will you achieve your vision? What parts of your function will you focus on and which will you leave alone? What does the overall business strategy demand in terms of areas to focus on? What objectives will be a priority for you and the team?

Share this vision with your team and your manager. Get them to test it for flaws and to make sure that they are comfortable with the aspirations you have expressed.

Week 6: Plan

Now start to consider the barriers to achieving your vision. Will you need to restructure? Do you need more skills or better capabilities in your team? Are the processes and systems up to it? Also think about the gap between where you are now and where you want to be (see Chapter 5).

Put together a high-level plan. At this stage, it does not need to be detailed, but it should provide a roadmap, stating clearly what you are looking to achieve. You will, of course, need to take time validating your plan with members of your team and your boss. Finish the vision by establishing clear individual and team expectations and performance measures.

As well as putting a plan in place for the team, think about the capabilities you personally need to build in order to successfully lead the team. Where there are gaps, create a personal development plan (PDP) to gain the necessary skills or experience.

Finally, at this stage, you should reflect on the new role and ensure that you are able to balance your work commitments with your preferred lifestyle. Encourage your team members to do the same. There is no point in doing a great job if you burn out in the next ten months!

By the end of Week 5, you will hopefully have done a great job, but you will also be pretty tired. Even the most capable and confident managers tend to use up a lot of nervous energy when getting stuck into a new job.

Use this week to take time to relax and get to know the team better. While you will already have started this process in Week 1, spend more time with each of them on a one-to-one basis and listen to their views, aspirations and concerns. Talk to each of your key stakeholders again and test the various elements of your vision, updating it as you go.

Pay particular attention to your boss and get to know him or her better, too. What is your boss's preferred leadership style, what are the major opportunities and threats and how does he or she feel your first five weeks have progressed?

During this week, make sure you get on top of your day-to-day administration and clear as much of your in-box as possible. Ensure that your email list is under control and take time to delegate non-critical tasks to members of the team as early as possible. Remember, it is much better to deal with issues early, before they become crises.

Week 7: Build your reputation

Recognise that your new role may be fundamentally different from your previous role and that, in order to succeed, you may need to do things differently. This is particularly important when it is your first role in management, as you will have switched from achieving results through your own efforts and expertise to achieving them through others. Remember that your personal reputation will now be dependent on the ability of the team to deliver results. Start to look outside your own organisation and identify industry best practice. Seek to understand how you compare with others and the best of the competition, and what ideas you can and should adopt.

Think about the different events you attend on a weekly basis, and how you should behave on each occasion. Check that you need to attend these and whether there are other meetings that might be more relevant. Think about what you can do to enhance your reputation as a professional. Think about what you will get out of each event, and ask what you can do to contribute. Perhaps there are opportunities for you to take more of a leadership role or facilitate others.

Your team members may well not report to you directly, but be functional specialists you must influence to deliver your vision. These 'virtual teams' are often more challenging to lead, so, in order to build your reputation, you may need to be sensitive to the needs of individual members and adapt how you work with them in order to get the best results.

Take time to build your network. The more senior you become, the more important your network will be to your future success. Your key contacts will initially be internal to the business, but, as you become more established, look outside the business at professional bodies. Be critical in terms of how you use your time as some of the network organisations you can join promise a lot but deliver little. As an effective change manager in the business, seek to identify and bring in novel ideas, new thinking and best practice from other organisations.

Week 8: Start the change process

Your early quick wins will have given you a feel for what is possible, but, more importantly, they will have helped to build your reputation as someone who gets things done and establishes relationships with key people across the business.

The longer-term and more substantive quick wins will be on their way to completion over the next few weeks. It is important to 'land' these achievements to start delivering real changes to your business results, so review their progress on a weekly basis. Make sure your team understands that these changes are critical to the future of the department and you see them as high-priority projects.

You are now beginning the process of significant change and development that will realise your vision. During this week, you can start to set the routine that will drive through the changes you want.

→ There will be a consistent simple message to communicate regularly to all stakeholders.

→ You should set up regular management reviews to monitor critical performance indicators, including project delivery.

→ Demonstrate the culture and behaviour that you want to see in others, whether that be entrepreneurial, decisive, rigorous or inclusive.

→ Consult Chapter 5 for guidance on implementing change.

Week 9: Reflect and learn

Now stop and review where you are. Take an hour or so at the start of the week to sit back and reflect on what has gone well, what has gone badly and why. Go back to your original plan or to-do list and tick off the items you have delivered against, then critically review areas where you failed to meet expectations.

Meet with your boss and ask for an informal review of your progress. Many bosses are not very good at doing formal performance reviews, but nevertheless it is an essential part of continuous improvement. Then meet with your other stakeholders and get their inputs regarding what has gone well and what they would like to see changed.

Week 10: Develop your two-year plan

Over the last nine weeks, you have built your reputation and credibility, developed important relationships with influential stakeholders and your confidence has grown. You will by now have an opinion on what you want to achieve based on facts and the advice of experts around the business. Now is the time to develop your two-year plan and seek to influence the strategic direction of the business.

A lot will depend on whether you are starting from scratch or taking over an existing team, but, in either case, start by reflecting on your earlier vision and update it if necessary. Then work back and identify what needs to be done and achieved on a month-by-month basis. Keep the plan for Year 2 at a high level, but plan the first three months in detail.

Once you have your plan, identify barriers or potential problems that could get in your way. What could go wrong, what could cause this to happen and what can you do to prevent it? Build these actions into the plan.

Finally, you should be as specific as possible about how you will know whether you are succeeding. Set KPIs you can monitor on a monthly basis that will let you and your boss know if you are on track.

Checklist: what do I need to know?

During your first ten weeks in a new job, start gathering information that will help you to deliver results, build your team and develop your career. Use this checklist to see if you have the necessary information – using a simple red–amber–green status, where red indicates major gaps in current knowledge and suggests that immediate action is required, amber indicates some knowledge is missing and may need to be addressed at some stage in the future and green indicates that you are on track.

TOPIC	INFORMATION	RAG
Business context	The major trends inside and outside the industry that will impact what you do and what you should be aiming for	
Business strategy	The overall vision and strategy for the business and how that translates into the part of the business that you're in charge of	
Team objectives	The KPIs that will be used to assess whether or not you and your team have been a success	
Stakeholders	Those individuals or groups you will work with and will influence the success or failure of your plans	
The team	Individual members of your team – their names, backgrounds and relative strengths and weaknesses	
Your area of responsibility	The main business processes you are in charge of, their strengths and weaknesses and the opportunities for improvement that you have identified	
Customers	Your top five internal or external customers and their specific musts and wants	
Suppliers	Your top five suppliers – who they are and how they contribute to the success of your team	
Your boss	Your operational manager – who your boss is, his or her preferred style and what it is that really makes this person tick	
Vision	A simply articulated and regularly communicated picture of where you want your part of the business to be in two to five years' time	
Implementation	An action plan and future expectations in terms of what needs to be delivered when, and by whom	
Budget	The budgets you have to work with – where the resources will come from, what the signing off process is and how the budgeting cycle works	
Resources	The people, facilities, equipment, materials and information available to you for your innovation activities	
Scope	The boundaries that have been set for you and your team – the things you are not allowed to do	
Key events	The major events and issues that are happening within the business that will influence what you need to do and when	
Potential problems	The risks you face going forwards – the things that could go wrong, based on the assumptions you have made	
Review process	The formal review process for your internal team reviews, at which KPIs will be reviewed with your boss	

STOP – THINK – ACT

Now put together a plan for your first ten weeks.

What should I do?	What do I need to achieve?
Who do I need to involve?	Who needs to be involved and why?
What resources will I require?	What information, facilities, materials, equipment or budget will be required?
What is the timing?	When will tasks be achieved?
	Week 1
	Week 2
	Week 3
	Week 4
	Week 5
	Week 6
	Week 7
	Week 8
	Week 9
	Week 10

Visit **www.Fast-Track-Me.com** to use the Fast Track online planning tool.

Models and frameworks for evaluating risks

Professor David Olson University of Nebraska–Lincoln

Without risk, there would be no motivation to conduct business. A key principle is that organisations should accept those risks that they are competent to deal with, and 'outsource' other risks to those (such as insurance companies) more competent to deal with them.

Enterprise risk management has always been important, but the events of the twenty-first century have made it even more critical. The top level of business management became suspect after the scandals of ENRON, WorldCom and other business entities. Financially, many firms experienced difficulties resulting from bubbles. The most spectacular failure in the late twentieth century was probably that of long-term capital management,[2] but it was only a precursor to the more comprehensive failure of technology firms during the dot-com bubble around 2001. The problems that can arise when cultures interact demonstrated the risk from terrorism as well, with various terrorist attacks, including 9/11 2001 in the USA. Risks can, therefore, arise in many facets of business. Indeed, businesses exist to cope with risk in their area of specialisation. Chief executive officers, however, are responsible for dealing with any risk fate throws at their organisations.

Risk management developed in finance, with growth in accounting being especially strong around the turn of the century. Financial risk management has focused on banking, accounting and finance. In addition to the core perspective relating to financial risk management, there also are perspectives relating to accounting, supply chains, information systems and disaster management. Aspects of risk, including information systems, disaster management and supply chain perspectives, have also been presented.[3] Risk management relating to natural disasters is also an area of great contemporary importance.

There are many tools available to assist in the evaluation of risk, including frameworks and controls in the enterprise risk management process with respect to supply chains, information systems and project management.[4] These can include decision analysis models, focusing on simple multi-attribute rating theory (SMART) models[5] to better enable supply chain risk managers to trade off conflicting criteria of importance when making decisions. These models only apply when trade-offs exist.

Monte Carlo simulation models are the obvious operations research tool appropriate for risk management.[6] Simulation models have long been applied in the valuation of risk, including supply chain contexts and the calculation of the value at risk. Simulations handle divers probabilistic factors, but, usually, they can't be used to optimise a situation.

There are also mathematical programming models, including chance-constrained programming,[7] which incorporate probability into otherwise

[2] Lowenstein, R. (2000) *When Genius Failed*. New York: Random House.

[3] Olson, D. L. and Wu, D. (2008) *Enterprise Risk Management*. Singapore: World Scientific Publising Co.

[4] Olson, D. L. and Wu, D. (2010) *Enterprise Risk Management Models*. New York: Springer.

[5] Mustajoki, J., Hämäläinen, R. P. and Salo, A. (2005) 'Decision support by interval SMART/SWING – incorporating imprecision in the SMART and SWING methods', *Decision Sciences*, 36 (2) pp. 317–39.

[6] Hoyt, R. E., Powell, L. S. and Sommer, D. W. (2007) 'Computing value at risk: a simulation assignment to illustrate the value of enterprise risk management', *Risk Management & Insurance Review*, 10 (2) pp. 299–307.

[7] Charnes, A. and Cooper, W. W. (1959) 'Chance-constrained programming', *Management Science*, 6 (1), pp. 73–9.

EXPERT VOICE

EXPERT VOICE

linear programming models and data envelopment analysis.[8] These models require specific sets of assumptions.

Additionally, business scorecard analysis[9] can be applied in the context of enterprise risk management.[10] Scorecards apply only to the measurement of performance.

[8] Charnes, A., Cooper, W. W. and Rhodes, E. (1978). 'Measuring the efficiency of decision-making units', *European Journal of Operational Research* (2), pp. 429–44.

[9] Kaplan, R. S. and Norton, D. P. (2006) *Alignment: Using the balanced scorecard to create corporate synergies*. Cambridge, MA: Harvard Business School Press.

[10] Wu, D. D. and Olson, D. (2009) 'Enterprise risk management: small business scorecard analysis', *Production Planning & Control*, 20 (4), pp. 362–9.

7

LEADING THE TEAM

The successful manager uses many tools and skills, but perhaps the most important is the ability to get the team to deliver. Whether it is through inspiration, delegation or relentless pressure to perform, the Fast Track manager will ensure that the team meets its objectives. To be an effective team leader, you will need systematically to understand your skills and key qualities – focusing on the key aspects of your management style that will enable your team to deliver.

Be what you need to be: be true to yourself but don't just be yourself

In terms of managing a team, it is easy to say 'be yourself'. It seems logical as trying to be something else will be difficult to sustain over a long period of time. Equally, pretending to be something you are not will put you under extreme pressure and potentially result in you being unmasked, just when it matters most!

Being yourself is not always an option, though. If your team is inexperienced or short on confidence, you need to demonstrate confidence and conviction. If your team is stuck in a rut, you will need to jolt people out of their routines. If your team is facing an uphill struggle, you will need to inspire and show a sense of realism. If your team is being asked to deliver a stretching target requiring long hours with potentially little reward and where they see you as the voice of 'management', you will need to be strong and forceful in the short term as well as showing an intelligent will to cooperate for the long term.

If you are none of these things naturally, you may have to learn, adapt and adopt the right persona for each situation. So, it may not always be possible to '*be* yourself' and that may be difficult, but, crucially, you must be *true* to yourself.

Identify your core values and make sure that the persona you are adopting as a leader is aligned with your own values. If you can do this, no matter how unpalatable the immediate situation, you will be reinforced from within by a sense of knowing that what you are doing is right and honest.

Know your values

How you lead will potentially change on a regular basis, according to the people, situation and goal, but your personal values will serve as a framework to guide the underlying motives behind your actions and decisions as a leader.

→ **Respect.** The extent to which you care about the impact of your actions on others. If this is one of your key drivers, your leadership style should always reflect the needs of others.

→ **Personal ambition.** The extent to which your career and the associated trappings of success are key factors in your being a manager. If this is one of your main drivers, you are likely to put goals, KPIs and recognition high on your agenda.

→ **Process.** The degree to which you feel that data, good order and a systematic means of delivery are essential to the success of any enterprise or team. If this is a key value for you, you will determine (by way of rational deduction) that any enterprise (or leadership style) is only worthwhile if it is underpinned by good sound process and logic.

→ **Social interaction.** The extent to which you decide that if something does not involve people and enjoyment it is not an effective way of motivating a team. If this is one of your key values, you may avoid any leadership style that sets you apart from the team and be unlikely to favour solitary tasks.

The above list of values is not exhaustive and not mutually exclusive. Most managers will recognise an affinity with more than one of them, but, equally, will feel most comfortable with maybe only one or two of these styles. The key to being true to yourself, and being the manager you need to be, is to identify which style is most suited to you and understanding how you can exploit that style to help your team deliver.

QUICK TIP **STOP WASTED EFFORT**
Stop people doing things that will not achieve your goals. In businesses, many people continue doing things that they think are important or have been told to do before, whether or not they matter now. This distracts valuable resources that should be focused on your goals.

Know your team – building alliances

Only a very strong, and potentially misguided, personality would intentionally ignore the commitment of the team, believing they can strong-arm their charges into effective delivery mode by a single-minded directional management (often with a good dose of fear thrown into the mix).

The intelligent Fast Track manager, instead, will invest considerable time and effort in developing working relationships with the following key team members.

→ **The vice-captain.** Having a second in command or a right-hand man or woman is a simple but effective means of ensuring that your message is still visible when you are not around. If this person is 'from the ranks' it also means, through them, you will be able to get an insight into the issues that may be affecting the performance of the rest of the team. This person will be able to help you delegate and manage delivery, freeing some time for you to focus on the bigger picture issues, such as strategy, value and external stakeholder management. You will not make the mistake of blaming this person for any lack of delivery – this is still your ultimate responsibility, for which you will gain credit or criticism according to your (team's) results.

→ **Functional experts.** Some people will be able to play any role, while others will be so specialist that those in them will be regarded as experts or gurus. Treat such people with the respect they deserve. Also consider ways in which their skills can be transferred or documented so that they do not become a single point of failure or a bottleneck.

→ **The awkward squad.** In some teams (especially those you may inherit), it is probably inevitable that certain players will be disinterested or, at worst, obstructive. You will not always have the option to ship these people out, so you need to either get them on board or minimise their potential negative impact. You may be able to marginalise difficult team members, but it can be better to bring them on board. They may not have bought into your strategy and vision, so you need to understand why. Meet with them and openly discuss your strategy and how this will affect them – can you build mutually rewarding objectives? Think also not just about conflicting objectives but also about different styles and values. If you value social interaction, but your 'rebel without a cause' is motivated by process and structure, think about ways you can harness this energy to deliver. If you can tease out an element of your strategy that will meet the drivers of a difficult person, it is highly likely that your difficult person will cease to be an obstacle and may even become an ally. This is easier said than done, though, so if their impact is endangering the team's objective, never forget the 'ship them out' option.

→ **Get to know the non-performers.** Let us look at an example. Rob had been appointed project manager for the roll-out of a new IT application to a global sales function. He soon felt that his training manager (Norman) was going to be an obstacle to success as his enthusiasm was non-existent and he seemed to feel that the whole project was doomed to failure. Over a beer, Rob discovered that Norman had been involved in a few projects that had gone horribly wrong. Norman felt that this project bore all the hallmarks of a disaster and didn't feel like being associated with it – he had plenty of other jobs to do.

Norman felt the software was not fit for purpose and he wasn't about to evangelise the new system on Rob's behalf. Equally, the target user group had been through enough changes of late and were likely to be unreceptive to another initiative from head office. Rob had no alternative to Norman so he set about bringing him on board.

→ He met the software team with Norman and reviewed the application and user input fields. Norman was right, the software *was* flaky and not really fit for purpose. A revision schedule was produced and Norman was made part of the user review team.

→ Rob organised stakeholder meetings with the managers of key users – both in person and by web-cast. He got Norman involved and helped him to see that this was not just another initiative but a mission-critical programme that, if successful, would change the way the business operated.

→ He reallocated budget to training to enable Norman to design workshops in locations that would motivate all involved.

→ He met Norman's boss to review Norman's workload and priorities. Norman's work routine was refocused on this critical project, including his annual appraisal and bonus.

→ Each of these activities helped, but, as a whole, they combined to make Norman feel he was an integral part of a project that really mattered. His commitment levels skyrocketed and, with a few other lucky breaks, the project – and specifically user acceptance – was a huge success.

QUICK TIP *SPONTANEOUS THANKS*
Arrange a night out on expenses (with permission if you need it). Give a quick, fun reward with the company putting its hand in its pocket to say thank you. There does not need to (should not) be a formal trigger for this – it is an impromptu, ad hoc idea.

Team types

Whether you are a first-time manager or an old hand, it still pays to reflect on the nature of your team and determine what the team needs from its manager to help members gel and deliver against key objectives. One size fits all would be great, but reality dictates that different leadership styles will be appropriate for different scenarios.

Team type	Issues	The ideal Fast Track manager
New and inexperienced	This team is facing a daunting challenge and the majority of its members are new to the business area and not sure what to do or when to do it – or even what success may look like	Be confident, focused and, initially, directive to get the team on the right track. Your roadmap needs to be simple and clear. Act as a sounding board and conduct regular fact-based reviews. Highlight some actual results and invite people to discuss what they think they have actually achieved. Keep your door open – literally
Exhausted	Having done a great job in difficult circumstances, this team is being asked to do it all again. The motivation of its members is on the wane – they can do it, but they're thinking, 'Is it really worth it?'	Show respect, being honest, open and realistic. Seek out those performing well, rewarding and promoting them as appropriate. Sustain their motivation by regularly highlighting and celebrating successes. Promote the team ahead of yourself when communicating achievements internally. Seek to rest, rotate and refresh where possible, even if this means taking risks. Freshen your people up. Is there room here to send them off as mentors and advocates to other teams?
Poor performing	This team keeps missing targets and deadlines. There appears to be a latent pool of talent, but nobody seems to be stepping up to the plate and mediocrity is seen as acceptable	Be data-driven. Only recognise poor performance where it is against agreed targets. When it is identified, analyse poor performance in the context of the environment in which the individual operates. Set clear remedial plans and agree them with the relevant team members. Highlight and reward examples of good performance. Why not have a performer of the month award (with a decent prize, such as dinner for two or case of wine) to highlight and drive improved performance

Team type	Issues	The ideal Fast Track manager
Virtual	This team scarcely recognises that it *is* a team – geographically diverse, it is easy to ignore other team members. The workload for all team members is way too high as most people are trying to do everything on their own and not sharing responsibility. They feel the virtual nature of their team means this is unlikely ever to change	Process will unify your team. The goals need to be clear, but, most importantly, the key players need to know how they should and can interact. Identify and communicate examples, synergies and teamwork. Design systems (IT, conference calls, meetings and so on) to maximise virtual interaction. Start by issuing an organisational chart for the team that also shows who owns which parts of the team deliverables
Entrenched	Been there, seen it, bought the T-shirt and thoroughly cynical. This team has outlasted countless new managers who have failed to make an impact – all the rhetoric about change and yet this team still does what it has always done. Its members aren't good or bad – they just don't need to change	Focus on change and results. Where relevant, introduce new systems and processes to deliver change in performance – critically (and unremittingly) disable old legacy systems and ways of working. Highlight and reward examples of adopting new behaviours and processes (even if associated results are yet to come!). Ask for new ways of reporting and encourage early adopters
Peer	The members of this team are all on a level, including the manager. They all know as much as each other and they all have the same power, so how will they respond to one of them being the manager?	Play it by the book and be creative. This is a real challenge to your skills as a solid manager with innovative tendencies. Fall back on your skills of setting visions and goals and managing delivery consistently. Avoid the trap of trying to micromanage or control your peers. Focus on deliverables, not managing others' styles. Get your peers on board, for example by instituting Monday morning meetings with bacon sandwiches! Give them a reason to be part of your team – sharing a few stories over a cup of tea and a bacon sandwich is a simple place to start

Team type	Issues	The ideal Fast Track Manager
'Them and Us'	The classic white-collar v. blue-collar scenario – management v. unions. You work for the same organisation and should have the same fundamental goals, but it doesn't feel like that!	Work at understanding the rewards and consequences of success and not just from your perspective. Understand the impact of delivering success on each party. Typically, disharmony can arise when one party feels that they are being asked to deliver with very little return. Ensure that the returns are appropriate and properly understood, ensuring buy-in from all levels. Show honesty and even-handedness by being prepared to get rid of people who are not prepared to play the game on *both* sides of the divide
Project	Project teams are all different, but they tend to have two things in common: they are (or should be) temporary and there is a mixture of levels, typically with a project manager whose job it is to manage people at a higher level in the organisation and probably not in the same area	As well as being goal-focused, the Fast Track manager will adopt an air of confidence, knowing what needs to be done, blended with a humility that comes from knowing that he or she will not deliver the project without the team. In this role, the ideal manager is an assiduous communicator – understanding the styles and preferences of each key stakeholder and adapting the message accordingly to ensure all people deliver on time and in full. Having a one-to-one with each key member of the team is essential to get this off to a good start

The characteristics of a great team leader

Do unto others … The role of a team leader is to maximise the results of individual contributions, ensuring that the combined output is greater than the total of the individual parts. Given that the team leader has to be a chameleon, capable of changing approach and tapping into different styles according to the needs of the situation and individual, it is useful to have a reference list of desired qualities that will be practised, honed and easily accessible to the Fast Track manager.

Patience – a game for more than one. Not everybody knows what you know; not everybody is as able and confident as you in a delivery situation. If you are going to ask people to deliver on tough tasks, make sure that you know their skill levels and be prepared to manage them through the task. If a manager is surprised somebody cannot deliver, it may be the case that his or her lack of understanding is to blame. Why would a new employee know how to deliver? Even managers have had to acquire knowledge over time – it is rarely innate. Allocate time and emotional energy in advance – it will get used as you facilitate your staff on their learning journeys. Such patience may require planning and you occasionally will have to steel yourself when the questions seem 'beneath you' or asinine, but the returns can be immeasurable. Your team members will be grateful for your quiet support, motivated to do more and help you get to the top.

Crisis, what crisis? Time is tight, the pressure is on, the report is (over)due, the numbers don't add up and your team is flapping. Joining in the headless chicken routine may feel hard to resist, but the Fast Track manager knows that it won't help the team and it certainly won't help him or her. Chesley Sullenberger, the US Airways pilot who landed his plane on the Hudson after a bird strike in February 2009 could have reacted differently, but joining the crew in a mutual prayer session *after* the event seems to have been the wiser option.

Wisdom. Knowing the answers is great, but knowing you don't have the answer is even more powerful. In management, wisdom is a practical not theoretical gift and, as such, it is often borne of experience. Being new or inexperienced, a Fast Track manager will wisely recognise the need to tap into other people's knowledge and exhibit a little humility in many situations.

Realism and pragmatism. You can't win every battle, some deadlines will be missed and not everybody will share your goals or enthusiasm. Accepting this and working out how to mitigate an imperfect world will help you to develop plans that actually deliver and, in difficult times, when the pressure is on, it will be a welcome reminder that you are human.

Idealism and ethics. Being an idealist and championing a cause sends a strong message to your team. You stand for certain unshakeable truths, which matters in a world where some people may just be out for what they can get.

Motivator. There are many schools of thought on the 'how to' and mechanics of motivation. Your approach will be dictated by your own personal style and the needs of the team. Whether you use the carrot or the stick is your choice – just don't forget to address this key area of team management. People need to be energised and inspired if they are to commit to your project. You can run the risk of allowing them to develop their *own* enthusiasm or take the proactive route and systematically align the team with your goals and beliefs.

Professionalism. As a team leader it is also important that you are perceived as being unswayed by emotion and you are prepared to stand apart from the masses. To do this, you will need to be able to call on your professionalism. In other words, you will know how to be consistent and play things by the book. When necessary, you will dress and act with an appropriate, understated conservatism. You will certainly not join in with the baying crowd. This may not be your style, but it is a useful card to be able to play. A simple way to develop a professional persona is to keep your own counsel – make people guess what you are thinking. You may have fun surprising them at a later stage.

Value aware. You know how to evaluate and recognise the value of all contributions, not just the big ticket items. This will earn you respect from team contributors, but it will also mean that you maximise the value contribution of all activities within your control, driving you and your team's results.

Manage, then do. The temptation for busy managers is to get their hands dirty, helping to deliver success by contributing to individual tasks. You may need to do this at some stage, but you are, first and foremost, a manager, a conductor of the orchestra. Your job is to create the right environment and a clear set of objectives against which others can deliver success. Analyse your time usage, dividing it into managing and delivery. If there is too much in the second category, you are either not trusting your people to deliver or they are not good enough. The situation must be rectified or you will stop being a manager. The conductor of the orchestra calls on the string section to lift the audience and the percussion to create impact, but could do neither if he or she ran around playing the stringed instruments or beating the drums. Similarly, a good project manager will coordinate the delivery of results. Software will be right first time, people will be trained and KPIs delivered – and all this while charming the sponsors and stakeholders.

Fun. Work is not a matter of life and death; it is much more serious than that. Well, actually it is not. Try not to be formulaic about creating a 'fun' environment (there is nothing quite as grim as planned spontaneity or simulated sincerity), but encouraging a smile – be it in the face of adversity or at a ten-pin bowling night – will not only help with team bonding but also go some way to creating a relief valve that kicks in when the pressure is on.

Science v. art. Management can be seen as a science until it comes to managing people, when – despite the best efforts of many gurus and psychologists – it has a tendency to imitate art, in that you can't manage all the variables (and probably shouldn't want to). In an ideal world, a 'how to' guide would explore the different triggers and scenarios that would necessitate the deployment of any of the above skills. In reality, experience will tell you when to use these skills – or when you should have used them! The trick in accessing these skills as a team leader is to be aware of them as a toolkit and consciously approach each scenario from a specific perspective. Be ready to change, but at least start off positively.

 CASE STORY *PEOPLE MATTER, JENNIFER'S STORY*

Narrator Jennifer was an experienced business manager who had been given a major new role within a global publishing company.

Context This company had an enviable reputation and brand. It was working in a number of highly profitable areas and all members of the team were energised with a real enthusiasm for what felt as much like a vocation as a job.

Issue The business was facing a real challenge – the digital revolution was causing panic in terms of its effects on the business model, yet the appetite for knowledge and learning was greater than ever before. How could these potentially conflicting scenarios be profitably resolved? The enthusiastic team members were beginning to get scared as revenues were starting to flatten out. Could they turn it round or would they lose out in the digital world? They needed to agree a new way forward if they weren't to be left behind.

Solution Jennifer asked her team members – responsible for a small but high-profile section of the business – to work with her on developing a strategy for the future. They set a vision and mapped out a future business model based on a comprehensive SWOT analysis of the market and their own skills. The result was a roadmap that belonged to the team and reflected its needs and beliefs and it had the maximum buy-in as each team member was able to sell the vision to other key stakeholders. The execution of the strategy was swift and effective and the business was able to capitalise on digital changes that had previously been regarded as threats.

Learning Jennifer recognised that she could not impose a strategy in such delicate times – nobody would buy into a vision that they felt didn't reflect their personal concerns. In this case, building a roadmap with committed people was crucial as this was a complex environment and Jennifer would have been unable to answer the technical questions for each area. A cosmetically appealing vision would not have been enough; it needed and received deep-rooted substantiation.

Kicking off – setting your team up to succeed

Equipping it for success. As a manager, you will have a budget and your team will be running on legacy systems and equipment. Having the right mechanics in place to ensure delivery is important, in that it helps to do the job. It is also potentially very motivating. Don't blow your budget on new laptops if you have other priorities, but remember that this is an important area to address at some stage.

Environment matters. Few people will consistently perform to their utmost in an environment that is not conducive to success.

It may feel like somebody else's responsibility, but a cramped, scruffy office is your problem when it impacts your team's ability to deliver. Again, it may not be your number one priority, but your people deserve to have the right working environment at some stage – plenty of desk space, good lighting, ergonomic seating, even decent company cars. You may not have much in the way of budget, but an idea may be to get some T-shirts with team logos. These won't break the bank, but could motivate the team and will also help create a sense of identity.

Team spirit. A truly egalitarian team will attract the best from each player – creativity in attack, a solid work rate and endeavour in defence. There will be a no blame culture that encourages people to take calculated risks and a mutual zero tolerance for any non-performance. Wow! Sounds like a big ask and it is. The Fast Track manager is anything but naive and knows that such a culture will not evolve overnight. It is a long-term undertaking and starts with you consciously displaying and promoting the right behaviours – and recognising, as well as rewarding, similar behaviours in others. Meanwhile, why not try to build a team spirit, just as they did at United Biscuits. Trying to build a sense of entrepreneurial fun is not an easy task, but they tried a few simple tricks that did at least get people smiling. People could put what they wanted on business cards, such as Barrow Boy (salespeople) or Grand Fromage (director). It was a little thing that made people chuckle and created a sense of unity around the strategy of being more commercial.

Ground rules. Explaining to people the dos and don'ts of timekeeping, permissions and reporting, for example, may all seem a little dull in some teams (especially new and large, diverse teams). It is essential to set the team's expectations, however, and it may as well be done from the start to create a standard. Not doing this will give some people carte blanche to do as they please, leaving others feeling that they are doing the right thing while they are getting away with murder. Tolerate this and you will create a two-tier system that divides your team. You could institute a system of fines, such as for when mobile phones ring during meetings.

Team meetings. Keep them sharp and focused. The golden rule for meetings is that they are driven by the objective, not the agenda. So, If you reach a resolution before the end of the agenda, don't be afraid to wrap the meeting up early. You will save time and everybody will be able to get on with business. The prerequisite for this approach is to actually set an objective. Many meetings have an agenda, but don't seem to have agreed in advance a firm end point. Avoid this.

Roles and responsibilities. Look at your team processes and projects and be as clear as you need to be about who does what and who will be accountable for ownership of the outputs (and quality or value-added) from your team. Always discuss and agree this with the individuals concerned and communicate it to the rest of the team. Ideally, you will be able to build critical areas of delivery and ownership into annual review and reward systems. Look at the annual objectives for key employees and check that they are all aligned with your strategy. Publicise the relevant areas (do not include personal details, such as salary or bonus or areas for personal improvement, though!)

Decision-making. Either you make all the decisions or you encourage others to make their own decisions as well. The latter route will free you up to manage the team, but is potentially risky. What if the decisions go wrong and jeopardise your strategy? The key to building a team that is a good decision-making unit is to give some clarity on the different types of decision. Making people recognise that they are actually facing a decision is a challenge in itself. Get your team members to ask themselves the following questions on a regular basis.

→ How much will the required course of action cost?

→ How many people will this affect (and at what level)?

→ Have we done this before (successfully)?

→ What are the implications of failure to deliver?

For each of the above, set clear criteria and or thresholds, such as cost or number of people affected. If the answer is below a certain level, the decision should be made and executed locally. If it is above a certain level, the owner should still do the deskwork and make recommendations, but you should help them to determine the final decision. Giving price discounts is a good example of this, where different levels of employee have different rights to give discounts.

QUICK TIP *NO SURPRISES, PLEASE*

Tell your team that you do not want any surprises. If something is going to go wrong, they should forewarn you if necessary. You don't want to go to a management meeting and be told that your team messed up its part of a major project! It may be unpleasant, but, if you know about it in advance, you may be able to develop a defence case.

Changing the team. This is a difficult but essential element of team management. If you want to drive different, better behaviours and results, you will need to change your team. This could be as simple as reallocating resources and management, but, to be truly effective, it will involve shipping people out and bringing in new blood. This will mean that the team has your people in it and less baggage. The risk here may be that the old team was performing really well and your decisions negatively impact performance. Be mindful of this risk (can you change some underperformers?), but go for change of some nature. If you do not do this, it will potentially always be the *old* manager's team, with you as a mere figurehead. A simple place to start could be to change the team's administrator. In some cases, this person can be a power-broker and a defender of the old regime. 'Well, that wouldn't have happened in Bill's time' is an oft-heard refrain from such entrenched diary managers. If these people are good, the organisation will easily find a place for them. Meanwhile, you get someone who you can shape according to your ways of working.

QUICK TIP *MANAGE CONSEQUENCES SELECTIVELY AND JOINTLY*

Do not try to manage and create positive consequences for *all* your reports. This can be a complex and time-consuming activity, so select those employees whose contributions are absolutely vital to success and work with them to understand their needs. Design the consequences accordingly and never do this work without consulting the person affected.

Investing in people. Coaching, teambuilding, skills development – these all cost time and money, but are essential tools for the modern team manager. Investing in people is a simple but effective means of rewarding and motivating good, keen team members. It is also a means of improving the performance of the lesser lights in the team. A little effort and some resources focused on these players will enable them to step up to the challenges you set. Having tried to address any gaps in skills and experience, if there is *still* a difficulty with performance, at least your next steps will not be seen as knee-jerk reactions, but the right and considered things to do for the individual and the team. It is easy to think about this area, recognise its potential importance and then do nothing. Schedule a review of people development options with HR as soon you take over and get a plan in place within the first two months. It may change, but at least you have set the hare running.

Career progression. We all hear about staff retention being a major driver and, in truth, you don't want to suffer from a high churn, constantly having to train and embed new employees. You don't have the time and results will suffer. As a Fast Track manager, though, you will be eager to promote new blood and this means being able to create the space to move others on. Assuming, at some stage, you are managing a team that is performing well, you will not have the option to move on dead wood – you will need to move on good people. It is essential to grasp this nettle. You will benefit from having a refreshed team and learning how (in a controlled way) to manage people in and out of key positions. Your team needs it too. People need to see that promotion is not an unattainable mirage and your top performers deserve the recognition of being able to move on and up through the organisation (they have careers, too). If these people are held back, they risk becoming stale or even embittered about the person they see as having blocked their careers. It is good for your career, too, to be seen as a net exporter of talent. It makes people want to join your team and senior management will recognise your contribution to developing the organisation's people.

Management development: how much is explained by culture?

Professor Chris Mabey Birmingham Business School, University of Birmingham

EXPERT VOICE

Every firm has its favoured approaches to management development. To what extent are these culturally determined? Attempts have also been made to apply cultural values to the design and delivery of training. The various training and development techniques used by organisations can be arranged on a spectrum from didactic (trainer-centred, low-risk, content-orientated) to experiential (learner-centred, high-risk, process-orientated). In cultural terms, didactic methods align with high power distance and strong uncertainty avoidance, while experiential methods reflect low power distance and weak uncertainty avoidance.

From this we might predict the relative appropriateness of development methods in different cultural groups. For example, a 'fishbowl' exercise might meet resistance and withdrawal in a Latin culture and a lecture in Denmark will quickly turn into a combative discussion! Managers in economically developing countries may be analytical and seek certainty while Anglo, Northern and Latin Europeans are likely to be intuitive and question norms and assumptions, thus undermining the power distance between trainer and trainee. To instil trust in the development activity, organisations in the latter cultures prefer high-level managers as instructors to hiring external consultants or trainers.

In a study contrasting leadership styles in the USA, Japan and Taiwan, the research team concluded that, in comparison with many other political and economic factors, culture is probably the most stable factor that drives management thinking and, hence, development. In particular, they found that the more a culture assumes human potential to be uneven across organisational members (as against 'talent' being uniformly distributed), the more likely leader training will emphasise specialised expertise rather than general management skills. An important caveat, of course, is that national boundaries may not always coincide with cultural boundaries. The same researchers established cultural heterogeneity (internal dissimilarities) to be highest in the USA and lowest in Japan.

It seems, then, that cultural context plays an important part in the priority given to management development in the first place, as well as how strategic or tactical it is considered to be. An understanding of cultural preferences also sensitises us to the *style* of such training and development – formal or informal, elitist or democratic, programmed or opportunistic and so on – that might be favoured in different countries. It also allows a degree of comparative cross-cultural analysis, which can inform the facilitation of learning processes from one country to another.

Such a cultural explanation has limitations, however. The tendency is to classify rather than explain. So, typologies of management development may be identified or preferred methods of development allocated to countries or country groupings, but this fails to actually explain a great deal. Invariably, we need to dig deeper into institutional arrangements, historical precedents in a given cultural setting or look for wider pan-regional dimensions, such as educational patterns or gender bias, to uncover why managers are developed in the way that they are. There are also dangers in treating culture and country as the same thing and, related to this, oversimplifying national culture and glossing over exceptions and contradictions, underestimating the variety of responses from individuals located in the same culture. Furthermore, cultural analyses often suffer from ethnocentric bias. This is because researchers or observers tend to impose their own predetermined dimensions of culture when examining and comparing practices across countries. Few studies have the luxury of multicultural teams, with researchers located within and investigating their own cultures from the inside. National culture explains much but not everything.

For a detailed analysis of the significance of management development in an international context, see C. Mabey and T. Finch-Lees *Management and Leadership Development* (2008, Sage).

8

GETTING TO THE TOP

The Fast Track manager has a goal and a strategy to reach that goal. Such a manager cannot or should not allow his or her life and career to drift along, but successfully manage them in the same systematic manner as the job itself. The Fast Track manager knows when the goal has been reached and will be able to set new and more stretching goals at each stage, each of which is aimed at one thing – getting to the top.

QUICK TIP STICK WITH IT
The key to successful leadership is to focus on the key elements and stick to them, repeating them often. People have a lot on their plates and need to know what's important.

Where exactly are you going?

We all aspire to different things, but, as a Fast Track manager, you will want a career that moves onwards and upwards with speed and alacrity.

A great number of managers don't have so much a career as a series of pay cheques – they have no grand plan, but accept progression at the behest of others. God or boss willing, their performance will be recognised and the pay cheque will swell as they rise through the ranks. Others make little or no progress, either because of their reactive style or they simply don't understand the need to manage their career progression and, despite being eminently capable, they are simply absorbed into an anonymous layer of middle management, never to emerge!

As master of your own destiny, you will not accept a random, reactive progression through the management hierarchy. Instead, you will determine your career objective in advance and all your professional actions and strategies will combine to accelerate the journey along the career path to your ultimate goal.

As a Fast Track manager, you will determine very quickly in your career what the endgame looks like:

→ CEO by the age of 45

→ head of a function or manager of managers by the age of 35

→ retirement by 55

→ formal recognition from the business of your contribution to its success

→ move onwards at least every three years

→ work for three global business in three different geographical areas

→ double your basic salary every five years.

All these goals are aspirational and achievable. None is materially any better than the other and each reflects the differing needs and drivers of the individual. Some reflect very high levels of self-confidence, while others are more grounded, perhaps reflecting the manager's sense of self-awareness – that is, stretching but not outlandish.

It should be observed that those goals with a timeline are different from those without one. Setting a date as well as an objective is a great way of upping the ante – no timeline means the impact of *not* achieving is less apparent. Brushing a missed deadline under the carpet is not so comfortable.

The key thing about a personal goal is that it is self-policed – it is your own personal KPI. If you don't deliver, nobody will take you to task except yourself. You can let yourself off, give excuses and explain away your lack of progress, but, when you look in the mirror, you will be your own judge. Were your goals too high or did you simply not perform?

Switch off the autopilot

If your ambition is to be CEO, it is unlikely that this will happen by accident. Everybody's career progression will be different, but it is a racing certainty that the majority of successful career journeys are the result of at least a degree of both planning and conscious decision-making.

How you get to your goal in five or ten years is often very difficult to predict and maybe only a clairvoyant or an idiot would describe each step of the journey in advance. You will be affected by changes in personal circumstances and external influences over which you cannot exercise any level of control.

To reach your goal there are two key elements.

First, remember your goal. This sounds self-evident, but, once you have determined what you feel is right for you, it is essential that you keep this front of mind. Make sure that you cannot and do not forget this is your objective. Write your goal in the front of your diary, set regular reminders in your diary, make it your screensaver, turn your goal into a mnemonic, buy a desk toy and name it after your goal. Do anything, but don't forget it and *do not* change it (well, OK, but only after genuine consideration of the rationale for change and having evaluated why your new goal is more appropriate).

Second, become a conscious decision-maker. Your journey will be a series of crossroads and the route you choose will determine how quickly you reach your goal or if you just end up in a dead end. Actually recognising that a situation requires a conscious decision is in itself very important. Passively allowing the autopilot to take you through the working week is tempting and, indeed, your job may have become easy and the routine you have delivering some good numbers to your boss may mean that he or she is quite happy. So, why change a winning formula? Well, if the formula is going to take you to your goal, don't. If your current approach is unlikely to help you take the next step, though, then you are facing a career decision.

Schedule your own personal career reviews in the context of your goal. Be tough on yourself and ask what immediate steps you can take to move on up. Schedule this at least every six months and don't just do it when you are approaching your annual review as a means of developing an expedient argument for a pay rise! Get the senior job and the pay rise will follow.

It will not be possible to 'schedule' some decisions. You will have to handle some decisions on a reactive, flexible basis. How do I handle a change of boss? How do I handle a poor-performing colleague? What can I do about a product that is proving difficult to sell? The decisions that each manager may make at each of these points will and should be different, but what should guide any of us in terms of criteria for evaluating different options is the impact the selected alternative may have on our career goal. In each decision situation, assess options A, B or C for likely impact on the goal and, given that the risks are acceptable, choose the option most likely to help accelerate the journey to the goal. In the worst case, choose the option least damaging to the goal.

Value creation

If your desire is to move up the career curve, this will undoubtedly be assisted considerably by evidence of your ability to deliver value.

Value is sometimes referred to as a vague black box concept that is hard to pin down, but it is actually very easy to determine for most managers. Value is the delivery of targets – ahead of or on time and within budget and at least meeting performance expectations.

The Fast Track manager will ensure that the targets are clear and agreed in advance, then systematically manage deliverables of success to ensure that value is delivered. Hitting stretching sales targets, high-impact product launches, simplification of internal processes, production line improvements – these are all good, clear examples of adding value. Work out what value you personally add and develop a plan to deliver it.

QUICK TIP *BE HONEST ABOUT YOUR VALUE*
Ask yourself, will key stakeholders be able to recognise what I do? Will they agree that my strategy will help them to move forward? If the answer is 'No', change your message or your strategy.

Here's a good target – help your boss to shine

So, you hit your targets, yet still you aren't receiving the recognition that your results deserve. This may seem unfair, but, in the end, the likelihood is that your targets were not the right ones.

If your targets are not aligned with those of your boss, even when you deliver, your boss will be at best ambivalent about your achievements. If you can make sure that each of your goals is materially linked to the ongoing success of your manager, then your results will be recognised, appreciated and contribute to your career progression.

At your annual review, consciously talk about the issue of how your targets address your manager's needs. If necessary or appropriate, discuss this openly and agree how you can ensure that your efforts are aligned with those of your manager.

QUICK TIP **MANAGE UPWARDS**
Keeping your senior stakeholders on board is as important as team commitment. Don't just communicate to them: set expectations, then they will come to respect you as somebody who values their contribution.

Sell your success, sell yourself

It may not be everybody's style or feel very comfortable, but, when you have delivered and created value, you owe it to yourself (and your career plan) to ensure that this is effectively publicised.

Can your results be mentioned in the corporate newsletter? Are there team or functional presentations? How can you ensure that you are put forward for recognition? In order to not look like a braggart and a self-publicist, it is a good idea to seek acknowledgement for your department as a high-performing team, then, as team leader, the halo effect will be very powerful.

The objective of selling your success is to create awareness of your abilities across the business and with other senior managers. Equally, if you do it cleverly – by lauding the team's contributions, for example, it positions you as not simply a one-man delivery machine but an effective manager of people. You will also look like a player who has the confidence to not hog the limelight but allow good people to shine, which is what a senior manager does. If you are to be promoted as a manager, this needs to be seen as a core belief underpinning your management style.

Your reputation precedes you!

Regardless of your results and how well you perform, it is often the case that you will acquire a reputation within your business that will determine your likely career progression. This reputation may be good or bad, it may be deserved or undeserved. As a Fast Track manager, you must be in control of your reputation. Get this wrong and the consequences for your journey to the top could be dire. Let's look at an example of how this can happen.

Mike had been a well-respected manager in a global business for nearly 20 years. He had successfully managed a range of functions in different geographical areas, and senior management clearly valued his creative enthusiasm for the next challenge. He was a role model for many – results-focused and healthily iconoclastic (unaccepting of restrictive corporate norms and ingrained ways of working). He breathed life into his projects and inspired all around.

Mike reached a crossroads, when he was passed over for a promotion to general manager. Frustrated, he set out to find out why. He was shocked and surprised to find that a senior manager from early on in his career had (without malice) given him a corporate reputation as a clever visionary but also as someone who 'might not deliver'. His 20 years of outstanding results proved that he *could* deliver, but his flighty reputation was so entrenched that his chances of landing the big job were virtually non-existent.

Ever creative, Mike set out to rectify the situation. Targeting the key stakeholders whom he needed to reconvince of his worth, Mike developed strategies that would align him and his abilities with their goals. In addition, he arranged a meeting with the senior manager who had inadvertently sullied his name.

On reviewing the situation, the senior manager was truly surprised at how misconceived her opinion was. She was equally surprised that her opinions had caused Mike such issues in his career progression. She agreed, as far she had influence, to support Mike in any of his future career aspirations and actually became a useful mentor.

All the while, Mike kept his focus on delivering results, in his own creative style. In less time than he expected, it paid off as, in the next restructure, Mike was given a new, more senior role.

Your reputation, then, is critical, so don't let it become a bad one. More importantly, don't let your reputation be a surprise to you. Keep your ear to the ground and regularly sound out opinions, developing action plans to enhance and sustain your reputation by aligning your results with those of the business.

QUICK TIP PRIDE COMES BEFORE A FALL
Make sure that you have your house in order and know exactly what you are trying to do before you push other people.

Be your own change accelerator

If you are very good at your job, it is likely that two things will happen to you:

→ you will be kept in your current position, churning out excellent results

→ you will be promoted and given new responsibilities.

The former may happen for several reasons:

→ your manager sees you as his or her banker – when all else is heading south at a rate of knots, your enthusiasm and ability to churn out target-busting results may just save the day

→ there is no other obvious opportunity open to you as far as your manager and the rest of senior management team are concerned as they aren't aware of your skills and desires

→ you don't push, asking for new challenges and horizons.

As a Fast Track manager aiming for rapid career progression, you will not accept stagnation – no matter how well you are performing. You will push for progress by:

→ setting yourself medium-term career progression targets, such as a maximum 18–24 months in any single role

→ mapping out career options – think about which functions you might move into and why

→ discussing your career thinking with management and HR – explain the implications (but not in a threatening way) of slow progression

→ networking on the back of your success – how your skills can be transferred/sold to other managers

→ where no clear options exist, identifying new projects, challenges or roles that could be created for you – such a role must add strategic value to the business and represent a means of accelerating the journey to your goals.

 CASE STORY NO LIMITS, PAUL'S STORY

Narrator Paul managed stakeholder relationships for a global food company. He was new to the business, but not the industry. An ambitious player, Paul wanted to keep moving up.

Context This global food manufacturer with multiple divisions (from drinks to snacks to restaurants and beyond) was acutely aware of the need to keep key influencers on board in order to gain support for its business activities. In Paul's division, the decision had been made to systematise the management of key stakeholders to ensure that support was maximised and potential blockers were 'brought on board'. If Paul could install his system elsewhere, the business would profit from it and he would be recognised as a pragmatic, results-focused manager – just what the business needed.

Issue Paul's division was doing a great job, but it represented only a part of the overall business. How could its results and systems be rolled out to the benefit of other parts of the business? Like many major corporations, each division was proud of its independence and didn't want to feel that it had to use other people's thinking. Also, to get anything moving across business units would involve entering a protracted, bureaucratic decision-making process.

Solution Paul took his division's solution to operational users in other divisions. He showed them the simple benefits, how to use it and how it worked in creating advocacy in key external stakeholder constituencies. He worked with these small teams to set up the system to meet their needs and 'held their hands' while they created a user base within their own divisions. The systems took off and each division adopted Paul's technology, saving time, effort and money and helping the business to build better external advocacy in each division.

Learning By rights, Paul should not have gone near this project. His boss was wary of the political ramifications and, if it had bombed, Paul (and his division by association) would have been the fall guy. Paul went beyond his 'decision rights' to create a solution for the group. The learning is that he did it in a way that, had it failed, would have stayed below the radar. Most importantly, he managed the risk of his journey (deliverables and people) to ensure that a great solution could be effectively moved on to a group level without jeopardising individuals. The key learning is to go for it but do *not* endanger other people's careers.

The need to conform

Conforming with the expected norms can take many forms and be restrictive, but, in other ways, it is hugely enabling.

Conformity can be about being dull and boring – slavishly adhering to a dress code and following the corporate norms, for example. Toeing the corporate line and being 'on message' seem to be ever more important in some sanitised corporate worlds where eccentricity and iconoclasm are seen as dangerous forms of anarchy that may poison the minds of innocent and compliant colleagues.

In some organisations, however, the norm can be that people be different, promoting independence, avoiding processes and dismissing the process-bound back office team. In such businesses or functions it has become the norm to view processes as emblematic of a dying world, despite the fact that, without them, the businesses would simply fail to function.

The truth of the matter is that rules and creativity need to coexist in a successful organisation. The same goes for the Fast Track manager. You will know when to keep quiet and when to break the mould. You will be expert at balancing these conflicting drivers. With an unremitting focus on your goals and how to maximise results along the way, you will exploit the status quo to support good performance, introduce new thinking and have the energy to accelerate when you need to.

The experienced Fast Track manager will exploit the norms and loopholes in an organisation to deliver value and maintain the journey to the top.

QUICK TIP *BE DIFFERENT*
It helps to stand out and be noticed – for the right reasons, of course! Think about how you will promote yourself with your team, your peers and senior managers.

Do I really need an MBA to succeed?

Your journey will be driven by your skills and the results you achieve. As a Fast Track manager, you recognise that your results will improve and your journey accelerate if you constantly strive to enhance your skills and abilities.

Investing in yourself is a vital element in becoming a successful manager – seek out a coach and mentor, internally or externally. In addition, consider the benefits of a professional management qualification, learning about the science of management. This will help you to be more successful.

Without doubt, a qualification such as an MBA is a powerful calling card. It sends positive signals to employers and commands respect among your peers. Remember to use such qualifications carefully, however. It is important that you are not seen as an MBA theoretician as, in the end, it's the results that matter. Equally, don't use it as a shield or a sword – don't hide behind it or use it to prove a point. Aim for achievements, using the MBA thinking to help you get there.

Promotion and pay

To many managers, 'getting to the top' is a combination of these two aspirational concepts and they are often seen as indivisible. In fact, failing to accept that you can have one without the other will reduce your options and potentially delay your progress. The Fast Track manager knows how to manage them separately.

If you are offered a pay rise without promotion, take it! Don't be fooled by the whiff of money, though, and don't let it change your goals. Settling for a pay rise is often the first step in abandoning your long-term aspirations, so take it for what it is, but don't become too comfortable just because you can now afford a skiing holiday and golf club membership.

Promotion is the key driver, whether or not it is associated with a pay rise. In an ideal world, clearly promotion, with its additional responsibilities and probably increased workload, should be accompanied by a commensurate increase in remuneration. This is not always the case. Sometimes an organisation tries to get more out of a manager for the same salary. Sometimes the organisation is offering the chance to deliver with a view to being remunerated accordingly when the manager has proved him- or herself in the new position. Neither of these is ideal, but each is sometimes understandable, depending on the business and the manager in question. If times are tough or if the manager is quite inexperienced, both situations may be quite logical.

The temptation may be to reject a promotion if there is no extra pay. Why accept the hassle and extra responsibility if you are not going to be paid for it? The Fast Track manager will rarely reject the offer of another promotion, even with the lack of financial reward. This will come. In the meantime, the promotion represents a chance to shine. More importantly, it offers the chance to leverage an increase in salary or bonus when the time is right. In the final analysis, within or beyond the current organisation, promotion represents a step up, which can be leveraged on the route to the top.

Easy money, hard promotion

Sometimes you will hit a target and be given a bonus, but promotion seems a much more elusive reward. This could be due to any number of reasons.

→ It is sometimes the case that it is easier to give people money than it is to give them promotion. Promotion may not be practical organisationally or your manager may see it as an undesirable complication if, for example, there is a series of stretching targets and finding a replacement for you is not going to make his or her life any easier. Either option may be all right in the short term, but, in the long term, you need to find a way out or get around the obstacle.

→ You may have earned your bonus in terms of delivering on objectives, but it may also be that the targets set were a little soft. So, you earned your bonus, but didn't earn shine in a way that encourages promotion. When agreeing annual targets, clarify how delivery will impact not just your bonus but also your career. If your function can't realistically offer an appropriate career path within a certain time frame, review the options with HR. Either way, don't accept patsy objectives if you want to be respected and given extra responsibility.

Moving out to move up

Will your goal be achieved by staying in the same company? A survey carried out in the USA revealed the following statistics:

→ most managers today will stay for an average of three to three and a half years before moving on to another job

→ almost 43 per cent of those managers left voluntarily to go to another organisation (looking for greener pastures)

→ nearly 27 per cent left voluntarily without having a job (that always raises an eyebrow)

→ 32 per cent left for other positions at the same rate of pay.

The evidence seems to suggest that moving on is an essential element in moving up. It may be worth looking around your own organisation at the history of senior management in order to understand whether or not your career goals are likely to be achieved in your current organisation. If a high number of senior managers have come from outside, then the likelihood is that the senior managers of the future will *also* come from outside. What does this mean for your chances of getting to the top? If the senior managers have all been developed in-house, this is great in a way, but it could also mean that they are unlikely to move on to another organisation to make space for you, so perhaps that is something you need to do.

Regardless of the make-up of the structure of upper management, there is still a rationale for moving jobs in order to enhance your prospects of career progression. Moving on gives you experience – experience of new structures, teams, issues and strategic environments. It potentially exposes you to new functions and responsibilities. It may even enable you to work in completely new industry sectors. This experience is not just critical in helping you to be a better manager but also a vital component, affecting the way you are perceived by other potential employers.

Moving on is fun. It can refresh a stale working routine and stimulate better performance. Who doesn't put in a little extra effort when starting a new position? The great, often unmentioned, benefit of moving on is that the new business often has little knowledge of your experience and will generally give you the benefit of the doubt, assume that you have great abilities (why else would they hire you) and promote you accordingly. What, honestly, would you have to do at your current company to give your career this kind of boost?

Let's look at an example of what can happen.

Charles was a really effective salesperson, but he was bored with his portfolio and felt distinctly undervalued, from a financial point of view. He also saw little chance of career progression, given the recent arrival of a new sales manager.

Charles quite easily found himself a new job in a new industry with better money and better career prospects. His old firm was shocked that he should want to leave. After he explained his dissatisfaction and reasons for wishing to leave, he was offered a 100 per cent pay rise and the new sales manager was fired, his position being given to Charles.

Charles accepted. He would rather that his success had been recognised without him having to force senior management's hand, but the new management position (not just the extra money) was too tempting.

Charles stayed for a further two years and helped the business to transform its performance by introducing a new key account management programme. The company tried again to keep him at that point when he accepted a new job, but there was no career move like last time, just a little more money. This didn't fit with Charles's goal of becoming sales director, so he moved on, with the blessing of the business.

Stop doing your old job!

'Well, it's great to be your new boss and I would love to come to the first team meeting, but I do have some commitments that I still have to fulfil back in Berlin, so I am going to have to pass. I am sure you will get on fine without me.'

Some managers, bizarrely, expect to succeed with a new team and a new challenge when their energies and attention are still partially devoted to a position for which they are no longer responsible or remunerated. For a very short period of time, such an approach may be laudable – you are helping out former colleagues. From a career and networking perspective this may be an intelligent thing to do, too, but, in the medium to long term, it can become a real problem.

Clinging to your former position sends out many messages – that you are afraid of leaving your comfort zone, have no vision for the new team, don't want to be with your new team, you are not aware of your limitations ... the list goes on.

The Fast Track manager stops doing the old job and focuses on the new position from day one. It may be that this is not practical or what the business wants, but, at some stage, you need to identify a cut-off point between the past and present. Managing with your eyes on the rear-view mirror cannot be tolerated on an indefinite basis.

Develop a proper exit strategy from your old job, clearly handing over ownership of key deliverables and exhorting your replacements to develop their own management philosophy. Make them understand that you will not be there to help them (not even by email). If you have been a good manager, your old team – having been briefed by you – will be confident and able to work on without you.

Do you really need to win the popularity contest?

As a Fast Track manager, you will manage many people at many different levels. You will network with many more. In order to reach your goals, you will need the active support of colleagues and contacts from various different areas.

The temptation exists to try and win the support of everybody by trying to be everybody's friend. Given that we are all different, this requires a lot of any one person. Being friends with everyone means being a person who is capable of establishing friendships with people at all levels and with all outlooks. A very few unusual people can do this, but, unless you are Nelson Mandela, with a seemingly unerring sense of what each person needs, you are not likely to succeed in being everybody's friend.

The Fast Track manager realises that his or her goal is not to be liked, but be respected. If you are respected, people will assist and promote your aims. People will also accept bad news more readily and go the extra mile for you.

Respect is earned, not given, and you achieve it over time. It starts with clarity of vision and consistency of values. Respect comes from results. You also gain respect by communicating with people according to their needs and their style, even when it is not your own. Your job may not make you popular, but how you do it will command respect. Achieving respect from peers and other stakeholders will be a key staging post in any journey to the top.

Networking

The Fast Track manager's abilities will be recognised as outstanding. It is, however, often as important to be recognised as it is to achieve results. If your face is known, for the right reasons, it is likely doors will be open to you that would otherwise be closed and you will be considered for opportunities not otherwise attainable or of which you were simply unaware.

It is unlikely that anybody who succeeds as a Fast Track manager will be a recluse. Rather, they will be successful external operators, capable of maximising and exploiting the connections within their environments to expedite progress towards a goal. Indeed, networking is the most efficient way to get yourself known, as well as to come to know the professional environment and key players who will be able to positively influence your route to the top.

Internal networking

Knowing the ropes is not just a metaphor for understanding the technical mechanics of a job. You also need to know how the politics of the organisation work and be able to play the game accordingly. Getting to the top will require you to understand the key players and develop an approach that will position you for success. How you go about maximising your position is a matter of personal preference, although arming yourself with some results is always a good first step. Knowing and being known by the major powerbrokers, though, is key.

The 'Look at me, aren't I brilliant?' approach is one way to be noticed. It can be a high-risk strategy, however – perhaps best avoided unless you have a sworn affidavit from the CEO to support your immodesty. Better options for internal networking include being part of internal groups (such as social or sports or work-related ones), getting on to strategic project teams, writing articles for the corporate newsletter and offering to arrange or get involved with a charity event.

External networking

Limiting your career and network to a single company will potentially restrict your growth opportunities. It will restrict your ability to learn and gain new experiences and, most importantly, will leave you exposed in times of need. Numerous otherwise excellent managers have seen their career stall because of a poorly developed external network. Let's look at a couple of examples to see just how important it can be.

No network Craig

After six years of devoted service to a single organisation, with every professional moment focused on resolving internal issues, Craig was asked to leave the organisation because of a group restructuring.

Craig had been vice-president for Europe for a €900m business, but, despite very costly outplacement support, he simply could not find a new opportunity commensurate with his skills and experience. His lack of an up-to-date network meant that he had nowhere to turn. Eventually he fell back on his old network and was able to develop a new business opportunity with some former colleagues, but he was unable to find a project at his true level.

Ad hoc network development

Nigel was vice-president for a global service function with profit and loss responsibility for in excess of €1bn.

After a restructuring left him without a position, he too struggled to find a new role via outplacement and his network was poorly developed. Again, he had focused on helping his team to achieve.

Realising that his history of senior management with a major player in a specific sector was likely to be of interest to other players in that sector, Nigel set about building an external network. He contacted and arranged lunch with the CEO of each of his former major competitors, in order to discuss issues and experiences in the sector. Three months later, Nigel had been promoted to the position of vice-president of strategy with global responsibility for mergers and acquisitions.

Having learned the lessons of seclusion, Nigel is now an assiduous external networker. It is not always easy, but the returns justify his efforts.

The benefits

External networking can be hard work and it can be difficult to do this in high-pressure environments. If you can find the time, industry-specific bodies and regular forums are a good place to start. If you can't do this, look at professional networking sites on the internet, such as LinkedIn. You can also network externally on a private basis via organisations such as the Rotary or Lions clubs or even the parent/teacher association at your children's school, which can also be good fun!

Experience shows that the network never dies. If you have a good relationship with somebody, chances are that 10 or 20 years later that person will still have positive memories of you and his or her door will still be open to you; don't be afraid to knock.

Finally, you *do* have a network, even if you are not aware of it. You may not have been *trying* to build a network, but everyone you ever met or interacted with represents a part of your network. This is always worth bearing in mind as you never know which email or phone conversation will potentially come in handy a few years down the line. It is perhaps not wise to become sociopathic about your interaction with each member of society, reviewing how you might be able to exploit them at some point in the future, but, keeping an effective, constantly updated address book will do no harm when you need to access a contact in a specific industry to progress your career.

Idea management

Professor George Tovstiga Henley Business School, University of Reading

EXPERT VOICE

What does it take for a firm to become the next Apple or Google? What are they doing differently to set themselves apart from thousands of others struggling to replicate their success? *Can* their success be replicated?

No doubt, many have asked themselves these questions and, no doubt, there are many possible reasons for the innovation success of these companies. While it is always perilous to attribute success to one factor or another, there does appear to be growing evidence that a few critical factors contribute to the success of these and other innovative high-flyers.

One of these has to do with the way in which they succeed in embedding the management of their ideas in a critical capability. Another relates to the organisational context and practices within these companies that support their capability.

Recent research by IBM, Innosight and the benchmarking firm APQC[1] confirms what experts have suspected for some time now – that the sourcing, shaping and realisation of ideas at innovative firms is determined by a self-

[1] Wunker, S. and Pohle, G. (2007) 'Built for Innovation', *Forbes*, 12 November.

reinforcing combination of culture and practices. Furthermore, the research identifies organisational forms that consistently nurture these activities.

Google typifies one such organisation. The company fosters a bottom-up approach to innovation. It makes no apologies for hiring the brightest, most creative people available. They are given ample freedom to experiment and lauded for coming up with ideas, which are quickly tried. Failure is expected – even rewarded – provided that it contributes to the firm's bottom-line learning experience.

A further attribute that sets firms of this type apart is their willingness to look outside their own organisational boundaries to find opportunities for new ideas. These might include partnering with other institutions, clients and other players, both upstream and downstream in their value chain. Once ideas have been scrutinised and assessed for their potential value, they are moved rapidly to market launch. The accelerated market launch characteristic of these firms is an outcome of their preference for validating ideas in the marketplace rather than with excessive upfront analysis.

So, clearly, bright, motivated people and organisations that succeed in unleashing their creative ingenuity – as well as a spark of happenstance now and then – are unquestionably part of the innovation success equation. Is this really all there is to understanding the success of the innovation champions, though? What if we could unpack the idea process of these organisations more precisely, perhaps by taking a glimpse into their enigmatic innovation 'black boxes'? What might we find?

Were we to peer into the innovation high-flyers' 'black boxes' we would likely discover how the innovation champions come up with their breakthrough ideas and nurture an uncanny awareness of strategic opportunities that remain obscure to their competitors. We would also find an almost ethereal intuition for ideas that have the potential to create fundamental and irreversible change on a global scale. Some of the things innovative high-flyers do appear counterintuitive and some of their practices clash with accepted management practices. It is precisely on this basis, however, that they differentiate themselves from the competition.

Peter Skarzynski and Rowan Gibson[2] argue that innovation champions arrive at their insights by virtue of their willingness and ability to:

→ challenge orthodoxies and deeply held prevailing industry logic

→ latch on to fundamental discontinuities that have the potential to substantially change the existing rules of the game and have gone unnoticed by others

[2] Skarzynski, P. and Gibson, R. (2008) *Innovation to the Core*. Boston, MA: Harvard Business Press.

EXPERT VOICE

→ nurture and leverage their organisation's strategic resources and capabilities in unique ways, of which idea management is a critical one

→ understand their market's unarticulated needs in ways that their competitors do not.

Each of these, while addressing a different aspect of idea management, might be considered a necessary precondition for innovation in its own right. The full impact of the four factors, however, unfolds when they collectively and in an orchestrated way constitute the organisation's fertile innovation context.

Is that all there is to it? No, there's more.

To discover new and unexploited opportunities, innovation champions build on their unique organisational context to venture beyond the conventional and explore uncharted territory. Innovators do this in a variety of ways. Robert Sutton's[3] research has led him to identify a few 'weird' practices of innovation high-flyers. Here is a sample of his recommendations.

→ Brainstorm a list of absurd things to do, reversing the ideas and developing arguments for and against each of these.

→ Brainstorm a list of ridiculous and impractical things to do, then develop the best arguments you can as to why you should probably be doing them anyway.

→ Use a devil's advocate and dialectical inquiry approach, challenging assumptions and decisions and alternately developing arguments to refute and support an idea.

The innovation success of companies such as Apple and Google, then, is an outcome of deliberate effort at building and nurturing an organisational context and practices that enable an unfolding of their idea management capability. I would argue that these are key factors, contributing to the fact that innovation at these and other innovative high-flying organisations is a way of life rather than an accidental occurrence.

[3] Sutton, R. I. (2002) *Weird Ideas that Work*. New York: The Free Press.

PART

DIRECTOR'S
TOOLKIT

In Part B, we introduced ten core tools and techniques that can be used from day one in your new role as a team leader or manager in your chosen field. As you progress up the career ladder to the role of senior manager and as your team matures in terms of its understanding and capabilities, you will want to introduce more advanced and sophisticated techniques.

Part D provides a number of essential techniques[1] developed and adopted by industry leaders – helping you to differentiate yourself from your competitors, both externally and internally.

	TOOL DESCRIPTION
T1	Organisational effectiveness audit
T2	Plotting your strategy: the strategy roadmap
T3	Executing your strategy: the project charter
T4	Building awareness: working with the Insights Discovery four personality types wheel

---

[1] All tools and techniques are available online at **www.Fast-Track-Me.com**

T1 ORGANISATIONAL EFFECTIVENESS AUDIT

Use the checklist below to assess the current state of your business. Consider each criterion in turn and use the following scoring system to identify current performance.

- **0** Not done or not defined within the business, unaware of its importance to management.

- **1** Aware of area, but little or no work done in the business.

- **2** Recognised as an area of importance. Some work done in this area.

- **3** Area clearly defined and work done in the area.

- **4** Consistent use of best practice tools and techniques in this area across the business.

- **5** Area is recognised as being 'best in class' and could be a reference point for best practice.

Reflect on the lowest scores and identify those areas that are critical to success and flag them as status Red, requiring immediate attention. Then identify those areas that you are concerned about and flag those as status Amber, implying areas of risk that need to be monitored closely. Finally, flag the remaining areas as Green to confirm that you are happy these areas of the business are under control at the moment.

The audit reflects the effective organisation model found in Chapter 4.

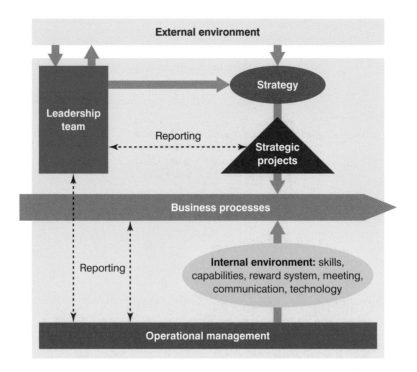

ID	CATEGORY	EVALUATION CRITERIA	SCORE	STATUS
P1	**Leadership**		0–5	RAG
A	Leadership team	An individual or management team is clearly charged with control of the business or business unit		
B	Inspiration	The behaviour and interactive style of the senior management team constantly reflect and reinforce the value and importance of the strategy		

ID	CATEGORY	EVALUATION CRITERIA	SCORE	STATUS
P2	**Strategy**		0–5	RAG
A	Vision	A vision is communicated that articulates clear business goals for a strategic time frame, based on an understanding of external markets and internal capabilities		
B	Strategic emphasis	A clearly articulated and communicated strategy supports decision-making in the business and enables operational drivers and strategic goals to be managed together without fundamental conflicts		
C	Resources	The business strategy can be and is used to prioritise resource allocation across different initiatives and projects		
P3	**Strategic projects**			
A	Prioritisation	A body or an individual exists to clarify project priorities across the business, ensuring that high-priority projects are given resources and lower-priority projects are slowed or cancelled		
B	Planning	A simple process for planning projects exists, which is widely used and all those involved understand how to use it		
C	Monitoring	Project progress (or lack of) is monitored at a sufficiently powerful level with the net result that projects deliver expected benefits on time		
P4	**Business processes**			
A	Identification	Key business processes are identified, have clear contribution to the value of the business and are well defined with clear responsibilities		
B	KPIs	KPIs link the phases and outputs of processes to vision and strategy and drive process performance improvement		
C	Performance improvement	There is a systematic approach (such as regular management meetings) to review KPIs and take action to improve process performance		

ID	CATEGORY	EVALUATION CRITERIA	SCORE	STATUS
P5	**Operational management**		**0–5**	**RAG**
A	Structure and definition	A clear management structure with clear individual roles is aligned to monitoring and continuously improving the business processes and the internal environment.		
B	Capability	There is a process for assessing individuals' capabilities and fitness for their roles before and during their tenure		
C	Information management	Information systems support the execution of the business processes		
P6	**Reporting**			
A	Full visibility and control	The management team has full visibility and control of all relevant business processes		
B	Alignment to KPIs	All reporting systems are aligned to the KPIs for the business		
C	Decision-making	Reported information is regularly reviewed and acted on		
P7	**Internal environment**			
A	Right skills	All staff and management have the right skills to deliver their roles and the business actively develops all individuals' skills		
B	Supportive culture	There is a culture that supports the goals and values of the business and encourages staff to work in the style required by the business		
C	Performance system	There is a reward and recognition system (not necessarily financially based) that encourages people to perform in their roles		
D	Learning	Insights and lessons learned are captured and used to improve processes and projects in order to maximise performance and avoid repetition of mistakes		
E	Meetings	Meetings have clear rationale, articulated objectives and agendas and are well run		
F	Communication	Communication is encouraged in all directions so that all those involved in the business know the vision and changes that may be affecting them		

To help you prioritise, generate an average score for each of the seven elements in the checklist. See the example below.

ELEMENT	SCORE	0	1	2	3	4	5	NOTES	ACTION (PRIORITY IN RED)	DEADLINE
Leadership	4.2					▣				
Strategy	2.1			▣				No clear strategy – people unaware of strategic direction	Run short off-site review to agree strategy and implications	By end March
Strategic projects	3.6				▣			Not enough people involved, so projects are not making good progress	Use above meeting to re-prioritise projects and agree how they will be delegated	By end May
Business processes	4.6					▣				
Operational management	1.3		▣					Some key managers don't appear to be up to the task	Review performance of key managers and set clear objectives with short-term deadlines	By end Feb
Reporting	2.2			▣				Paper-based and inconsistent	Get one of the team to investigate and implement automated reporting	By end March
Internal environment	1.2		▣					Very poor meetings culture	Get HR to run a very brief 'effective meetings' workshop	By end Feb

In your organisation, the whole is only as good as each individual element. If one link in the chain is weak, then the company will not operate to optimum efficiency and there is an increased risk of failure. The action plan, therefore, should be to focus attention and resources on the elements of greatest weakness first, then move the whole framework to a level of excellence. This approach optimises the use of resources and sets up a process of continuous improvement.

In the example above, the managers conducting the organisational effectiveness audit have identified that the weakest link is that of the internal environment used (average score 1.2). The plan therefore focuses initially on this area, with specific actions identified. Once the management team has increased confidence that the internal culture (in this example) has improved, the next stage would be to focus on the operational management and strategy areas and for these, too, actions have already been identified.

Under some circumstances, such as an initial concern about the maturity of the management team, you may decide to do this exercise on your own. There are two good reasons for involving others, however:

→ they may have valuable inputs that will help the assessment process, especially if they have observed this part of the business in action for longer than you

→ if you involve the members of your management team, they are more likely to buy into the outputs and commit resources to resolving the identified issues.

You can use this tool early in your appointment to a new role or as a trigger to energise change if you have been in the role for some time and need a new approach to stimulate some action. Re-analyse with this audit on a regular basis (every 12 months, for example) to monitor your progress.

If strategy turns out to be one of the areas you need to work on, too, look at the next tool, T2 Plotting your strategy: the strategy roadmap.

T2 PLOTTING YOUR STRATEGY: THE STRATEGY ROADMAP

Strategy comes in many forms, but the term generally applies to the process you use to set your vision and goals and work out how you will develop your piece of the business over the next few years. This strategy roadmap will help you to avoid the pitfalls and accelerate your journey towards your vision.

Let's think, first of all, about the value to be had from developing a strategy. Here are some of the key benefits:

→ creating a clear vision and strategic direction shared by the whole function or organisation that can act as a basis for positive communication

→ providing a context for a strong business performance, structural and investment decisions and business priorities

→ forming the basis for implementation, outlining the key projects required to promote change and gaining the commitment of resources to bring about their delivery.

As you go through the strategy process, a number of things will become more clear:

→ the current and future internal and external competitive environment – what our competitive strengths and weaknesses are and what changes we anticipate, what our customers will want

→ what the 'hard choices' are – which products or services or markets or customers should be emphasised or de-emphasised to best capitalise on the future environment

→ the strategic goals – what you can deliver in the strategic time frame, what you want to achieve and by when

→ the strategic implications – what will hamper you, internally and externally, what needs to be put in place to deliver the goals (for example, structure and responsibilities, business processes, infrastructure), and so on

→ the strategic projects – what the key strategic programmes are that will deliver the strategy, who will lead each one and how progress will be monitored.

The strategy roadmap

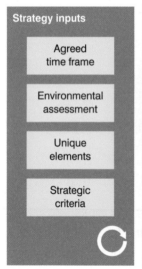

This diagram sets out the different phases of a strategy:

1 **Strategy inputs** – gather the information and opinions that will form the basis of the strategy

2 **Strategy articulation** – set out clearly the direction and goals for the business

3 **Strategy implementation** – organise the delivery of the goals.

The circling arrows in the diagram indicate that there is regular refinement of the strategy that you develop. This will happen as you go through the strategy process, learning more as you go and incorporating that into the strategy. There'll also be a need to review the strategy on a periodic basis to make sure that it still meets the needs of the world you made assumptions about before. The strategy development process ranges, in its fullest form, from an exploration of the environment in which the business is placed through to the execution of the strategic projects.

Let's look at each phase in a bit more detail.

Strategy inputs

Agreed time frame

To provide a point of focus and a target for implementing the strategy, set a time limit in which to achieve the strategy. The time frame can be guided by the speed of change within the industry, practicality and the ability to visualise. Typically this will be three to five years – short enough to make predictions, but long enough to stretch your thinking beyond what you can plan.

Environmental assessment

This is a comprehensive review of a range of factors affecting the business or your part of the business now and in the future. It gives you a complete understanding of and agreement to your internal strengths and weaknesses and the external threats and opportunities, so as to make informed decisions about the strategy. A SWOT analysis is a typical tool to use for this.

Unique elements

These are the unique or powerfully competitive features of the business from which a strategy can be built. You can identify them by looking at what has worked well in the past, where you have differentiation in the market and your competitive strengths.

Strategic criteria

List the criteria that will drive your choice of strategy in this part of the roadmap. This can be a powerful exercise to do with a team as it will tease out the existing values of the business as well as helping to clarify the attitude you want for the business going forward. You may end up with about five or six criteria, such as the following.

We will choose a strategy that:

→ increases profitability on our trading to fund business investment

→ attracts funding to enable growth

→ builds on and exploits our brand most effectively

→ meets the needs of our stakeholders.

Strategy articulation

Vision and strategic goals

Include a vision statement to communicate effectively the future direction of the business. This will be based on and may include a high-level description of the products or services the company will be selling and to which markets (if necessary, what products, services or markets it will no longer be operating in as well), plus specific business goals that everyone should be aiming to deliver.

Business matrices

If further depth is required (such as when thinking about a whole business rather than a function), this can be illustrated in matrix form to show the areas where future business will come from. To enable plans to be produced to achieve the strategy, develop matrices showing the products and markets that are emphasised in the strategy and those to be de-emphasised or discontinued.

Performance measures

To plan effectively and to track the success of your strategy implementation, set targets for revenue and other measures expected by function, business unit, product, market or year. You will need to consider the resources available and your stakeholders' expectations. The balanced scorecard approach may be valuable here.

Implications and implementation issues

You are now beginning the transition from vision and strategy to execution – actually delivering your vision. To do this effectively, you need to think about the implications of your strategy. What will hamper us, internally and externally? What must we build to deliver the goals (such as structure and responsibilities, business processes and infrastructure)? What are the key strategic programmes that will deliver the strategy? Who will lead each one? How we will monitor progress?

The output you are aiming for from this process is a list of strategic projects that will deliver your strategy.

Strategy implementation

Strategy implementation is one of the toughest things for a manager to do well. As you emerge from your strategic thinking process, you will very likely have a long list of significant things that need to be changed or introduced. You will also have no resources allocated solely to strategy implementation – people and funds will be allocated to operational jobs somewhere in the business. So, you have to overcome the challenge of lots to do and no one to do it.

Strategic projects

As you come out of the strategy articulation phase, you should be starting to build a list of the projects and initiatives that will need to happen to realise your strategy. Chances are that this list will be quite long and daunting. The key to success is to focus on a few at a time.

So, first, prioritise your projects on the basis of their current and long-term impacts. Take the top six projects to focus on initially and give each of them a project manager. Get the project managers to use the charter in T3 Executing your strategy: the project charter, next, to develop project goals and plans. Set up a regular (probably monthly) meeting to review progress on the projects and help project managers resolve any issues they come up against. Demonstrating your commitment to these projects by making this meeting a priority is essential. If you don't, your project managers will spend all their time on their operational roles and your projects will not progress.

As you move forward, some projects will be completed and new projects can be got underway.

Communication

We'd recommend that one of your initial projects concerns communication. It is vital that all those directly impacted by your strategy understand what you're hoping to achieve and how you want them to behave to make it happen. Communication will be a mix of telling people, involving them in interpreting the strategy for their roles and rewarding them for doing the right things. You'll need to repeat the message regularly before it will be fully accepted.

Review process

Remember that your strategy is based on your best estimates of and your assumptions about the future of the sector you are operating in. This is normal, but you should recognise it and conduct periodic (probably annual) reviews of your strategy to make sure that it still meets your predictions about the future. While a well thought through strategy will not need complete revision, it is likely that some refinements will be made in the light of new information about the environment.

T3 EXECUTING YOUR STRATEGY: THE PROJECT CHARTER

Building your vision and strategy is one thing – often fun and energising – but delivering it is something else. Strategy execution requires planning, prioritisation and perseverance.

Having understood your ability to deliver a strategy, overleaf is a powerful project charter template for managing strategy delivery with a completed example following it. The art of managing projects at this level is to have a clear overview of where they are going and not inundate your team with documentation that adds unnecessary work. Keeping this kind of paperwork to one page, more or less, will give you much of the control you need without overloading those around you.

Strategic Project Charter

Project title and goal	What goal, need or activity will be delivered and by what date?			
Project manager	Who is responsible for making the project happen?			
Date		Version		

Background and strategic context	What business needs are driving this project or what issues does it aim to overcome?
	How is it aligned to the organisation's strategy?
	What links or dependencies exist?

Target project benefits	Objective	Measure	Target
	What are the major deliverables or outputs?		
	What results will the project deliver or contribute?		
	How will the objectives be measured?		
Scope	What assumptions or constraints exist? What lies outside the scope of the project?		

Project activities resources and responsibility	Activity	Due date	Responsibility	Resources
	What major activities must be completed?		Who will	Who or what
	What are the significant milestones?		take charge?	is required
	What significant decisions must be made?			

Stakeholders	Stakeholder (group)	Influence (H/M/L)	Support (+/−/?)	Communication plan
	Customer			How will negative stakeholders be managed?
	Sponsor			How can you build on positive stakeholders?
	End-user			
	Resource provider			

Risks	Mitigating action	Responsibility
What might go wrong	How can you prevent or otherwise manage it?	Who will take charge?

Project team	Project sponsor/originator	
	Project team	

Strategic Project Charter: 'Green Pac'

Project title and goal	Project 'Green Pac' To introduce a recyclable blister pack by end Dec 2010 within budget €240,000
Project manager	Gareth Jones

Date	15 April 2010	*Version*	1.1

Background and strategic context	Corporate strategy to increase level of recyclable components in packaging materials
	Innovate in both packaging and delivery systems to increase competitive advantage
	Reduce reliance on metal-based (foil) packaging components

	Objective	Measure	Target
Target project benefits	Increase number of recyclable packaging components	20% increase	2011
	Reduce costs of metal-based packaging	15% (€20k)	2011
	Improve eco-friendly credentials of company	Survey	Quarterly
	Comply with government, EU and FDA legislation/regulations	Review	Ongoing

	Activity	Due date	Responsibility	Resources
Project activities resources and responsibility	Blister pack design (beta) proposal produced	30/8	Design manager	Design department
	Trial packaging production	30/9	Production manager	Line 1 (night shift)
	Decide optimum package design	14/10	Project manager	Board members
	Press release approved	30/11	PR manager	Press department
	FDA approval	30/11	Production manager	FDA consultant
	Initial production run	31/12	Production manager	Lines 1 and 2

	Stakeholder (group)	Influence (H,M or L)	Support (+ or – ?)	Communication plan
Stakeholders	Consumers	L	?	End-user survey via clients
	Suppliers	M	–	PR plan and account managers
	Production team	H	+ (low)	Change notes and strategy document

Risks	Preventative action	Contingent action	Action list
FDA delay decision	Advanced warning action document produced	Carry production packaging material stocks at +10% for Q1 2005	PR and production departments to lobby FDA with proposal documents on monthly basis
New packaging materials not liked by end-user	Carry out user survey trials in advance using third-party consultants	Limit new packaging to prescribed drugs only	Consultant with prescribed agencies (doctors) in advance (PR)

Project team	Project sponsor	Simon Derry (MD)
	Project manager	Gareth Jones

T4 BUILDING AWARENESS: WORKING WITH THE INSIGHTS DISCOVERY FOUR PERSONALITY TYPES WHEEL

Each person in every organisation is unique, bringing different styles, needs, motivations and expectations. In these differences are great strengths but also potential areas for conflict and disagreement. Insights Discovery is about understanding these differences and understanding more about yourself, others and how to build on them to achieve your goals.

Your view of everyday events, people and even world events is coloured by your internal beliefs. Your hero is someone else's villain, a colleague will ridicule your solution to a problem . What makes something right for you but wrong for others? To connect with others, you must start to see things from their points of view. The purpose of this section is to give you a tool for recognising personality traits in yourself and others and using that information to make the best connection with the other person, ensuring that, whatever the transaction – a sale, performance review or perhaps an interview, for example – it goes as smoothly as possible.

Insights Discovery uses the language of colour as a framework to explore the energies that interact within the personality as an aid to understanding yourself and others.

At its basic level, there are four colour energies.

→ **Cool Blue** You tend to be a little introverted and have a desire to know and understand the world around you. You like to think before you act and maintain a detached, objective stand-point. You probably value independence and intellect. You prefer written communication, to maintain clarity and precision, radiating a desire for analysis.

→ **Earth Green** You tend to be somewhat introverted, focusing on values and depth in relationships. You want others to be able to rely on you. You may defend what you value with quiet determination and persistence. You prefer a democratic style, valuing the individual and radiating a desire for understanding.

→ **Sunshine Yellow** You have a preference for extroversion and are radiant and friendly, usually positive and concerned with human relations. You enjoy the company of others and believe that life should be fun. You approach others in a persuasive, democratic manner, radiating a desire for sociability.

→ **Fiery Red** You have a preference for extroversion and have high levels of energy. You are action-oriented and always in motion, positive, reality-orientated and assertive. You can be single-minded as you focus on results and objectives. You approach others in a direct, authoritative manner, radiating a desire for power and control.

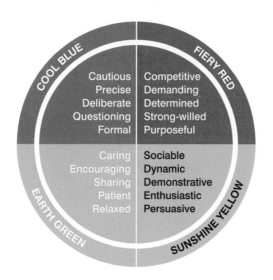

You may already have a sense of where you feel most comfortable on the colour wheel above. Certainly, you'll know which colour energy is *least* like you and, from that, you can reasonably assume that the *opposite* colour energy is *most* like you. You will, of course, have all the colour energies in you in differing amounts, so you may be able to relate to at least three of the colour energies moderately well.

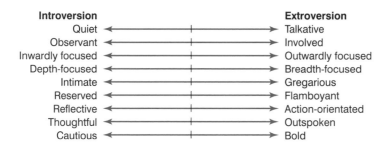

In assessing yourself or others, consider initially the attitude chart, above. If you or the person you are thinking about is talkative, expressive and bold, he or she is likely to be extrovert, so on the right-hand side of the Insights wheel – that is, with high levels of Fiery Red and/or Sunshine Yellow energy.

If you consider yourself or them to be observant, reserved and reflective, you are likely to prefer an introvert style and will be positioned on the left side of the wheel – that is, Cool Blue and/or Earth Green.

Now have a look at the list of decision-making functions below. Some people are formal, analytical and objective – they have a high 'thinking' function and will divorce decision-making from feelings. They occupy the top of the Insights wheel and will tend to have high Cool Blue and/or Fiery Red energy.

Others prefer to consider the impact of their decisions on people. They may appear informal, personal and relationship-focused, as well as, perhaps subjective and illogical. They will occupy the lower end of the wheel and will tend to have high Earth Green and/or Sunshine Yellow energy.

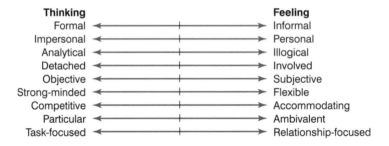

Thinking		**Feeling**
Formal	←——————→	Informal
Impersonal	←——————→	Personal
Analytical	←——————→	Illogical
Detached	←——————→	Involved
Objective	←——————→	Subjective
Strong-minded	←——————→	Flexible
Competitive	←——————→	Accommodating
Particular	←——————→	Ambivalent
Task-focused	←——————→	Relationship-focused

By analysing yourself or others on these two scales – extrovert v. introvert and thinking v. feeling – you can build a picture of where you or they may fit on the Insights wheel. For example, a high 'thinking' extrovert will most likely lead with Fiery Red energy.

When trying to identify traits in others, we can also get clues from body language, verbal style and even the working environment. For instance, someone who talks loudly, gestures, makes full eye contact and has a somewhat disorganised desk (to your eye, not his or her) is likely to have high Sunshine Yellow energy.

Once you know who you're working with, think about the most appropriate style to make the conversation run smoothly and for you to get the best result from the meeting.

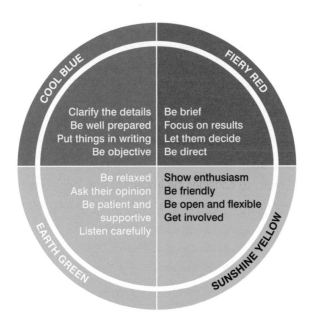

→ Those with a Cool Blue preference like a formal, businesslike atmosphere and would like your approach to be objective and task-orientated. They like to understand the logic and process – the *how* – and won't be rushed to a quick decision. Send them data beforehand (if possible) and expect them to need time to think over your proposal.

→ Earth Green energy prefers the company of other low-key, friendly people who demonstrate a genuine attitude of honesty and sincerity. They like a bit of informal discussion and worry about being taken advantage of so will shy away from apparently aggressive selling styles and 'hard closes'. Silence or an unenthusiastic response does not mean they reject your view.

→ Those leading with Sunshine Yellow energy like an open, extrovert, friendly and enthusiastic discussion and enjoy personal stories and distractions, so be prepared for a long, chatty meeting! Present to them with strong recommendations in an energetic style. Don't expect total truthfulness as they may wish to protect your feelings.

→ If you have Fiery Red energy, your motto might be, 'Be brief, be bright, be gone'. They like a businesslike atmosphere in which they feel that they are in control of events and hate to waste time. They will make decisions quickly when they understand the high-level benefits and won't want to know the details.

Being aware of others' styles and preferences will give you a distinct advantage in your dealings with them. Put yourself in their position, work on their terms and they'll come round to your way of thinking much more readily.

In summary, think about the following questions in the light of the above.

→ What have I learned about myself?

→ What do I appreciate about the styles of others?

→ How will I adapt my behaviour?

→ What is my key action?

THE FAST TRACK WAY

Take time to reflect

Within the Fast Track series, we cover a lot of ground quickly. Depending on your current role, company or situation, some ideas will be more relevant than others. Go back to your individual and team audits and reflect on the 'gaps' you identified, and then take time to review each of the top ten tools and techniques and list of technologies.

Next steps

Based on this review, you will identify many ideas about how to improve your performance, but look before you leap; take time to plan your next steps carefully. Rushing into action is rarely the best way to progress unless you are facing a crisis. Think carefully about your own personal career development and that of your team. Identify a starting place and consider what would have a significant impact on performance and be easy to implement. Then make a simple to-do list with timings for completion.

Staying ahead

Finally, the fact that you have taken time to read and think hard about the ideas presented suggests that you are already a professional in your chosen discipline. However, all areas of business leadership are changing rapidly and you need to take steps to stay ahead as a leader in your field.

Take time to log in to the Fast Track web-resource at **www.Fast-Track-Me.com**, and join a community of like-minded professionals.

Good luck!

OTHER TITLES IN THE FAST TRACK SERIES

This title is one of many in the Fast Track series that you may be interested in exploring. Whilst each title works as a standalone solution, together they provide a comprehensive cross-functional approach that creates a common business language and structure. The series includes titles on the following:

→ Finance

→ Innovation

→ Strategy

→ Sales

→ Marketing

→ Project Management

→ Managing People & Performance

→ Risk Management

GLOSSARY

Ansoff matrix A strategic diagram of product and market segments that illustrates, among other things, areas for growth, maintenance and decline in the future business

Balanced scorecard A tool used to track progress against a series of pre-set business measures or key performance indicators (often strategic). It is 'balanced' because it uses metrics relating to people development, operations and strategy, as well as finance. Can be further enhanced to see performance of a whole team or even the business on a single page

benchmark An approach to comparing performance (process, project, team or individual) with what is considered standard best practice. Benchmarking is driven by metrics such as cost, cycle time, productivity or quality

budget The amount of resources available to support delivery of a goal. A budget can be measured in financial or human resource terms

budgeting The art or science of managing resources in a proactive manner, such that shortfalls can be avoided or mitigated and sequencing of spending is matched to the rate at which the budget funds are released

career path A journey from first pay day to retirement that is managed by systematic means to reach a certain goal or position. This is opposed to a reactive worklife journey that reflects the ebb and flow of other people's decision-making

cash cow A significant revenue generator in a non-growth segment, the profits from which are either distributed externally or internally to support growth in other areas. For example, *The Sun* newspaper is a cash cow that enables News International to invest in digital news media

change The process of evolution that underpins the continued profitability of any enterprise. If a business stands still, either its customers will move on or its competitors will move in. No change ultimately means a fall in volumes and margins

coaching The use of (external) support to help a person develop his or her full potential. Generally applied when a person is promoted to a new, more demanding position. It can also be a remedial step to kick-start a change in behaviour

consultants Typically, external thought leadership human resources who will challenge ways of thinking and help the senior management team to develop new strategies and aligned implementation plans. A consultant should not be viewed as a 'pair of hands', brought in to alleviate workload or manage through a period of change

continuous improvement Ongoing efforts to improve products, services or processes to deliver incremental improvements over time – typically a cycle of plan, do, check, act

contractors Hopefully, inexpensive but experienced human resources who can fill a short-term gap to enable delivery of a project. Ideally, these people are not deployed within processes as they can become expensive fixtures. The beauty of contractors is that they usually have more flexible conditions, but beware as employment law is regularly changing

corporate coolade A liquid version of a corporate brainwashing mantra. Drinking this stuff is potentially dangerous and can seriously impair your ability to think as an individual (common sense and sense of humour will start to wane)

cross-functional A key characteristic of any truly effective project or corporate initiative. It should be designed by multiple functions with a clear understanding of the benefits and issues that each function will experience as part of the project

decision rights The restrictive framework within which you are allowed to operate and make decisions. Budgetary or hiring decisions, for example, may go beyond your decision rights. Set decision rights so that people know their limits and to clarify expectations

delegation Getting other people to deliver because that is the best use of their time and enables you to make the best use of your time

deliverables Where the rubber hits the road – tangible pieces of work that add value by themselves or pave the way for strategic and operational success

ERP Enterprise resource planning (ERP) is normally a software system (series of applications) designed to integrate all the information and functions of a business or company from shared data stores

ethics, corporate The basic beliefs of the organisation or team that guide its actions and decisions. Fair trade is a good example as that ethos ethically drives all sourcing activity

executive summary A one-page overview of a situation setting out all the key aspects and developments associated with a particular business issue. A useful tool for securing buy-in from people who will do not have time or who will be switched off by reading a wordy presentation or report

exit interview A meeting held with a departing employee to establish the rationale for their departure. Rarely done effectively, these are a tremendous opportunity to learn lessons and avoid potentially losing other good people

feedback The breakfast of champions! Feedback is a vital tool for securing input regarding what is being done well or badly. It should be designed/ given in such a way that it sustains good performance or changes poor performance

FTE Full-time employee – a person who is part of the team headcount. FTEs are unlike contractors in that they are a relatively fixed overhead. This means that they can be counted on if you need them to work on a task, but they cannot be switched off like a tap to reduce costs if times are tight

function and silos A team or department within an organisation that is responsible for delivering the outputs associated with a certain aspect of the business – IT, sales, marketing and so on. Some functions can be run as independent units with little interaction with other functions and these are regarded as work silos

Gantt chart A graphical representation of the sequencing of deliverables of a project over time. It was developed by Henry L. Gantt during World War I to help schedule the shipping of munitions from the USA to Europe to support the war effort

gap analysis An understanding of the different levels of performance

– where a team/function *is* versus where it *needs* to be and the size of the gap between the two points. Typically, a gap analysis may also include some form of recommendation on the work required to bridge the gap

HR Human resources – a function that delivers increasing value along a spectrum from organising simple, routine tasks (such as sick pay, holidays and car policy) to driving the human and intellectual capital of the organisation, articulating stretching new strategies and building people's capacity to deliver

impact A noticeable difference – ideally positive and achieved as a result of planned actions

KPIs Key performance indicators – the standout metrics that are looked at to confirm good or bad performance. These can be either for the business as a whole (BSkyB is driven by average revenue per user, ARPU, for example) or for specific functions or processes, such as the productivity of a manufacturing line or performance v. sales targets

management levels The hierarchy of an organisation is sometimes formally divided into set management levels, and promotion is viewed not in terms of function or responsibility but progression from one level to another. Such systems tend not to be very common as they are seen as restricting entrepreneurial egalitarian thinking. They are typically still to be found in large, denationalised businesses and quite regularly in big corporate businesses in the EU, especially Germany

MBA Master of business administration – a qualification (usually as a second degree) based on giving students an insight into the theories and practices of management across a range of disciplines, such as finance, marketing,

human resources, operations, process design and so on. The objective of an MBA is to make the student a more rounded business professional, able to understand the drivers and issues of each business area and, therefore, move into management positions in different parts of a business

mentor An experienced (usually internal) senior manager who acts as a guide to newer, less experienced managers, challenging their thinking and helping them to become more mature, successful managers

milestones Intermediate measures of success – staging posts on the way to successful delivery of a project. Milestones can be ad hoc to check progress ('Where are we, guys?' is a good question to ask after three months of frantic action) or planned ('Where will we be by Christmas?' or the annual sales conference could be a milestone during the roll-out of a new CRM platform, for example)

morals Your personal sense of right and wrong. Not formally an integral part of a management structure, but if your morals are questionable (non-existent), developing consistent loyalty may be tough

network All the people you have ever met, no matter how fleetingly. Those in your network may be more aware of you than you are of them

networking Getting out from behind your desk and meeting people – inside and outside the organisation

NPD New product development

operations The day-to-day running of the business and its functions

opportunity cost Doing anything within a work context costs, in terms of time and other resources. Using time and resources for a new opportunity means that another aspect of the business will be starved of those resources. Will the new project offer a higher return on investment than the other or will the cost of this new opportunity outweigh the benefits that could have been reaped by focusing elsewhere?

organisational structure – flat An organisational structure with only a few, often (deliberately) ill-defined levels, designed to encourage fluidity of information exchange and decision-making

organisation structure – hierarchical An organisational structure with multiple, clearly defined and consistently articulated levels, designed to bring formality, consistency and rigour to information exchange and decision-making

organisational structure – matrix An organisational structure (flat or hierarchical) in which an employee will typically have more than one boss and set of objectives, often designed to ensure that, for example, functional and geographic goals are both addressed by same person. It is important that the goals set by each boss are not conflicting!

ownership The intellectual claim on a key element of business strategy or the operational responsibility for a specific deliverable within the business, such as a task, process, project

pay scales Levels of pay, often associated with or determined by the management level at which an employee is working

performance management Managing (and rewarding) people or functions according to quality of output – not just for attendance

performance system A person's working environment, which can often have an influence on his or her ability or desire to do a good job

portfolio management Managing a range of events, projects or tasks according to a set of common criteria in order to help prioritise and monitor progress of more than one aspect of business performance

process A repeating sequence of actions designed to deliver a specific output. Given its repeat nature, a process can typically be measured according to efficiency (output per consumed resource)

product market matrix A matrix with products (existing, evolving, new) on the Y axis and markets (existing, evolving, new) on the X axis. The matrix enables a business to understand which services are delivered to which markets and can be used to determine future directions or strategic opportunities

project A relatively complex (one-off) initiative or series of actions designed to deliver a specific tangible output, typically time-bound and with a known allocation of resources

project management A structured approach to coordinating the deliverables of a project to ensure the maximum value is created to meet the (ongoing) needs of key stakeholders

promotion An upward move within the corporate management structure. Regular promotion is regarded by many as the key indicator of career progression

recruitment Bringing new people into the team to either provide additional resources to handle a greater workload or help develop new strategies and fresh ways of working as a means of accelerating the journey towards strategic success

retention Keeping a winning team together by retaining key players is a key management skill. The main tools used to achieve this are tailored reward and recognition programmes, as well as clearly mapped career pathways for your top performers. The latter recognise that they will move on at some stage, but, ideally, when you are prepared for them to do so

reward, management by A token of recognition. A reward is only a reward if it is seen as such by the recipient. A manager's preference for, say tickets to the big game – no matter how expensive – may not be a received as intended

risk management A structured approach to eliminating the causes of potential problems *and* planning mitigating actions to minimise the impact of a problem should it happen. The best risk management programmes are committed to paper (or use a web-tool) and the outputs are integrated into business-as-usual, not stored in a dormant file on somebody's C drive

scenario management A simple method for evaluating options based on constructing and evaluating the likelihood of the working scenario into which the solution will be launched. Scenario management looks at the effects of changing the levels of certain variables (such as costs, time scales, resources), assesses probability (high, medium, low)

skill development – facilitation One-to-one or group facilitation is often used to transfer a skill and, simultaneously, realise a level of value (practical ROI) for the team. A risk with facilitation is that the team members take a back seat and ownership remains with the facilitator

skill development – training Training workshops are a quick, simple and relatively inexpensive tool for transferring new skills into a workforce (for topics such as negotiation or project management). Care must be taken to incorporate and sustain learning to ensure that it does not remain theoretical, but can be transferred so it is of practical value

SMT Senior management team – typically managers of strategic functions or business units who are responsible for setting (and delivering) strategies

span of control The amount of time given to somebody before he or she is asked for an update on progress

sponsor A senior manager (or funding customer) who is motivated by the output of a project and who will help clear obstacles to ensure effective execution

stakeholder management A structured process for ensuring that stakeholder buy-in is maximised, typically by means of consultation and trying to ensure that their needs are addressed

stakeholders Any person or group of people affected by or having to live with or use the outputs of a piece of work

strategic charter A simple one-page document setting out a vision, the KPIs and key enablers/deliverables. Used to review strategic goals, track progress and sell a strategy to stakeholders

strategic time frame The time frame set for planning and realising a strategy. This is dictated by the pace of change in the business, but is typically three to five years

strategy The structure that will serve as a guide for all actions

SWOT analysis Analyses strengths, weaknesses, opportunities and threats as the basis for understanding a working scenario and developing steps to improve operational or strategic performance

systems The enabling mechanics that businesses use to automate and drive the efficiency of processes and other operational tasks (typically, nowadays, these are IT-related)

tactics The on the ground actions that are guided by a strategic framework and, if effectively executed, will deliver the corporate goals and vision

team A group of individuals with a common goal who recognise the importance of each individual's contribution to achieving that goal

trust The conviction that a person's actions can and will take your needs into account

value (proposition) The positive impact you will have (or be perceived to have) on the business and your working environment

vision A simply articulated and regularly communicated picture of where you want your part of the business to be in two to five years' time

white space The hand-off point or interface between two elements of a process that can often be poorly understood or unclearly mapped, resulting in confusion and delay. *See also* ownership

INDEX

Page numbers in **bold** relate to entries in the Glossary

EVERYTHING YOU NEED TO ACCELERATE YOUR CAREER

FAST TRACK TO SUCCESS

978027371992 2

978027372176 5

978027371990 8

978027372180 2

978027372178 9

978027371988 5

978027373290 7

978027373288 4

978027373286 0

A complete resource to get ahead as a manager – faster, bringing together the latest business thinking, cutting edge online material and all the practical techniques you need to fast track your career.

FT Prentice Hall
FINANCIAL TIMES